An Introduction to Primary Mentoring

Trisha Maynard

CASSELL

Cassell
Wellington House
125 Strand
London WC2R 0BB

PO Box 605
Herndon
VA 20172

First published in 1997

British Library Cataloguing-in-Publication Data
A catalogue record for this book is available from the British Library.

ISBN   0304 700460 (HB)
        0304 700479 (PB)

Typeset by:
   The Bill Gregory Partnership, Polegate, East Sussex

Printed and bound in Great Britain by:
   Redwood Books, Trowbridge, Wiltshire

Contents

Acknowledgements

We would like to express our gratitude to the Paul Hamlyn Foundation and the Esmée Fairbairn Charitable Trust for generously supporting our research. We would also like to express our thanks to the Welsh Office who chose us to undertake the 'Subject-based mentoring in the Primary School' project. We gratefully acknowledge the contribution made by all those who became involved in our research at the University of Wales Swansea. In particular we would like to extend our thanks to the teachers and student teachers who were so honest and forthright in their comments and so astute in their evaluations of the subject mentoring activities we devised. In addition, we would like to thank the staff and pupils of Manselton Primary School, Pen Y Fro Primary School and Ysgol Login Fach for allowing Mike Punter to take photographs of mentors working with student teachers in their schools. Finally, our thanks go to Michael Rowe for sharing his expertize on student assessment, to Rhiannon Jenkins for her invaluable comments and suggestions and to Illtyd Lewis for translating the subject mentoring materials into Welsh.

Introduction

In recent years all those involved in initial teacher training have recognized the need for schools to be actively involved in the professional preparation of teachers. School experience is no longer seen as an opportunity for students to put into practice understandings previously gained in higher education institutions (HEIs). What students can learn from working in schools – that is, what they can only learn from working in schools – and the unique contribution that teachers can make to students' development is now widely recognized and valued.

The role of schools in the initial training of teachers has been formalized in DFE Circular 14/93 (WO 62/93). This Circular stipulates that from September 1996, primary initial teacher training (ITT) courses must be planned and delivered in partnership between schools and HEIs: the curriculum for these courses prescribed as a series of government-defined competences on which students must focus for the whole of their training. Circular 14/93, then, gives schools the opportunity to take a key role in the professional preparation of the next generation of teachers.

Many schools have already begun working with HEIs in a more structured and systematic way and different models of 'partnership' are currently being developed. Some schools appear to be opting for a minimal involvement in partnership arrangements: for example, by undertaking a small number of student observations and contributing to the assessment of students' competence at the end of their school experience. Other schools are welcoming the opportunity to make a much greater contribution to ITT by:

- making regular assessments of students' developing competence;
- running school-based seminars;
- interviewing prospective students;
- contributing to students' college-based studies and to the planning of ITT courses etc.

The focus of this handbook

The particular focus of this handbook is on the specific contribution that teachers can make to students' school-based learning. Establishing successful partnerships with HEIs and effectively structuring and managing students' school-based learning, requires teachers to develop new knowledge and skills. This is very challenging and time-consuming. It appears to us that, at present, much of this learning is proceeding through trial and error. This handbook, therefore, aims to:

- Support schools in establishing and maintaining effective partnerships with HEIs;
- Offer guidance on developing effective mentoring practice; and
- Suggest activities that could be used by mentors to structure their work with the student teachers on placement in their schools.

Importantly, the suggestions and activities incorporated in this handbook are based not only on our own experience of working in different partnership schemes but also on extensive empirical and theoretical research. In writing these materials we have drawn, in particular, on the findings of three research projects, based at the University of Wales Swansea.

Three research projects

The first of these projects, 'The Role of the Mentor in Initial Teacher Training', which ran from 1992–1993, was funded by the Paul Hamlyn Foundation. This project initially focused on the developmental learning needs of student teachers and how these needs change over time. A second phase of this research explored in more detail two issues that assumed importance at different stages of students' development:

- class management and control; and
- lesson content.

As part of this project we also considered how the development of student teachers' professional knowledge could most effectively be promoted by teachers acting as mentors.

A second project, undertaken between 1993–1994, was funded by the Esmée Fairbairn Charitable Trust. This research was part of a larger project which involved six universities in the UK: the University of Wales Swansea and Oxford, Manchester Metropolitan, Keele, Sussex and Leicester Universities. The Swansea project, 'Effective Mentoring in the Primary School', focused, principally, on the process of mentoring subject knowledge in the primary school. This included an exploration of primary school teachers' attitudes towards subject knowledge and the challenges and demands of working with colleagues and with student teachers. A further aspect of this research was to examine the perspective of headteachers and their interpretation of the mentoring role, particularly those headteachers working in small schools.

The third project built on the findings of the two previous projects. As noted earlier, Circular 14/93 stipulates that ITT must be planned and delivered in a partnership between schools and HEIs. More specifically this Circular recommends that schools play a greater role in the preparation of students to teach the core subjects of the National Curriculum. Recognizing that schools and HEIs would benefit from the availability of materials to support subject mentoring in schools, the Welsh Office invited all HEIs in Wales to tender for a project aimed at developing and disseminating such materials. In July 1994, The University of Wales Swansea was notified that it had been successful in its bid. In this project, 'Subject-based mentoring in the Primary School', which ran between September 1994 and December 1995, eight primary teachers worked collaboratively with lecturers from the Primary Post Graduate Certificate of Education (PGCE) course to devise a series of activities aimed at developing students' knowledge, understanding and skills related to the teaching of the core areas of the National Curriculum.

The structure of the handbook

The handbook is divided into two parts, each part written by a different group of authors. Part A, 'The Principles and Processes of Mentoring', draws extensively on findings from the first two projects while Part B, 'Subject Mentoring in the Primary School: The Core Curriculum', represents the outcomes of the third research project. Part A incorporates Sections 1–4 and Part B, Sections 5–10.

Section 1 – sets out basic guidelines for headteachers who are considering becoming involved in initial teacher training or who are in the early stages of setting up a partnership arrangement with an HEI. This section deals with the preparation of colleagues and with establishing, managing and evaluating a partnership scheme. While this first section is addressed specifically to headteachers, the rest of this handbook should be read widely by all staff who are likely to become involved in working with student teachers.

Section 2 – outlines some of the basic strategies and techniques that mentors can use in working with student teachers – for example, student observation and collaborative teaching. This section also includes advice on the induction of students and how to run school-based seminars effectively.

As noted earlier, research by two of the authors suggests that learning to teach takes a particular developmental form; students pass through a series of 'stages'.

Section 3 – outlines a mentoring scheme based on the idea that, student needs will differ at each stage of their professional development and that the mentoring they receive should vary in aim, emphasis and approach in order to meet those needs.

Section 4 – focuses on student assessment and gives guidance on different strategies that may be used to assess students' practical teaching competence.

Section 5 – addresses key questions relating to the introduction and implementation of subject mentoring in the primary school: the demands of subject mentoring, for example and how this work might effectively be organized within the primary school.

Section 6 – consists of six activities that are intended to provide students with an introduction to good primary practice. These activities may be appropriate to the early stages of students' school experience.

Sections 7, 8 and 9 – include subject specific activities – eight activities for each core curriculum area. These are, in general, rather more complex and challenging than the activities in *Section 6* and might, therefore, be most appropriate for use on students' penultimate or final school experience.

Section 10 – uses extracts from the piloting of six of the above activities, to highlight key themes or issues that are likely to be of significance to the success of subject mentoring in the primary school. This section may be used as a resource to develop greater understanding of the significance and implications of this work.

Partnership language

In writing this handbook we are aware that as schools and HEIs have begun to develop different models of partnership so they have also begun to develop their own partnership language. Different terms are used to describe the various participants in the training process – for example, mentor, teacher mentor, class mentor, class teacher, senior mentor and the like. In addition, the roles and responsibilities of these participants have been interpreted in different ways. It is important, therefore, from the outset, that we clarify the particular terminology used in this handbook.

When student teachers are on *school experience*, class teachers traditionally have taken on the role of supervisory teacher: informally guiding students' development in ways that personally make sense to them. But where teachers are working with students in a more formal, active and structured way, we would maintain they have taken on the role of class mentor. The role of the class mentor is considered in more detail in Section 1.5.

As the involvement of schools in ITT has increased and the challenges and possibilities of mentoring student teachers recognized, many headteachers have chosen to appoint a designated *senior mentor*. This person, usually an experienced teacher with some managerial responsibility, is given the task of planning and co-ordinating student teachers' work within the school – for example, deciding in which classes student teachers are to be placed, supporting colleagues in their work with student teachers and

liaising with the HEI tutor. There is an exploration of the role and responsibilities of the senior mentor in *Section 1.4*.

Subject mentoring is rather different. The role of the *subject mentor* is
to focus specifically on the development of student teachers' knowledge,
understanding and skills in the teaching of one or several of the National
Curriculum subject areas. While this role is fairly easy to define, it is much
more challenging to implement within the primary school! *(Who* might
take on this role and *how* subject mentoring might be organized in the primary school is addressed in *Section 5.*)

Finally, we do recognize that while primary schools may have common
purposes and practices, they will vary a great deal in ethos, size, the
resources available to them and the aims and ideals of their staff. We also
recognize that some schools may be forming partnerships with more than
one HEI. In this handbook we try to take this variability into account. We
do not intend to advocate any one model of 'partnership'. Rather, our aim
is to enable schools, whatever the extent and nature of the contribution
they choose to make to the professional preparation of teachers, to form
more successful partnerships with HEIs and to be more effective in structuring and supporting student teachers' school-based learning.

Trisha Maynard, University of Wales, Swansea

Part A

The Principles and Processes
of Mentoring

**Edited by John Furlong, Trisha Maynard,
Sheila Miles and Margaret Wilkin**

Section 1

Initial Tasks for the Headteacher

1.1:   A statement of interest

Traditionally, class teachers have taken on the role of supervisory teacher to the students on 'teaching practice' in their classes: informally guiding students' development in ways that personally make sense to them. But DFE Circular 14/93 (WO 62/93) recommends that schools take a much more active role in the professional preparation of teachers. This Circular stipulates that primary initial teacher training (ITT) courses must be planned and delivered through 'partnerships' between school and higher education institutions (HEIs). While schools are under no obligation to become involved in partnership schemes, many *are* choosing to do so:

> If you are considering becoming involved in a partnership scheme then what are the initial issues that need to be addressed?

Some suggestions:

Talk to the HEI

You may be approached by an HEI that wishes to discuss the possibility of partnership with your school. Alternatively, you may decide to contact an HEI with which you would like to consider forming a partnership. In either case you will initially need to consider the HEI's interpretation of 'partnership' carefully and the degree of involvement and commitment you wish to offer. For example:

- Is the HEI offering open and equal negotiations?
- Does it already have a model of partnership in mind?
- Would that model be appropriate for your school?

Familiarize yourself with the appropriate documentation

– Government regulations

Headteachers should familiarize themselves with the appropriate govern-ment regulations. Part of DFE Circular 14/93 (WO 62/93), *The Initial Training of Primary Teachers: New Criteria for Courses*, is reproduced on pages 85–87.

- OFSTED/OHMCI

As part of the inspection of HEIs, all schools participating in partnership schemes will be subject to regular inspection by OFSTED (Office for Standards in Education) or OHMCI (Office of Her Majesty's Chief Inspector of Schools) for their work in initial teacher education. Inspection schedules are continuously being updated but it is likely that there will be an evaluation of:

- the suitability of the school for training purposes;
- the preparation of mentors;
- the quality of support by HEI tutors;
- the assessment of students' teaching competence by the school and HEI;
- the effectiveness of the partnership; and
- the quality of training in the school.

HEIs should be able to provide you with details of the current frame-work for inspection of primary ITT. It should be noted that, in Wales, schools inspected by OHMCI will be evaluated on the quality of their part-nership arrangements with initial teacher training institutions.

Make an initial statement of interest to the HEI

If you decide that you wish to explore the possibility of partnership in ITT further, you should make an initial statement of interest to the appropri-ate HEI. You will then need to begin preparing the school for partnership.

1.2: Preparing the school for partnership

Before becoming a partner in the initial training of teachers, there are a number of issues that can usefully be addressed by way of preparation. For example, you might:

- clarify the aims of student teachers' school-based learning;
- review the school's strengths and weaknesses as a context for supportive learning; and
- establish a proper basis for partnership with the HEI.

(A): THE AIMS OF STUDENTS' SCHOOL-BASED LEARNING

If your school is to become involved in the professional preparation of teachers, you are committing your staff as a whole to participating in that task since students will come into contact with and can learn from many staff members: teachers, nursery nurses, support staff etc. If there is agreement among staff on the aims of professional preparation, then the quality of training available to students will be enhanced.

How can staff explore and clarify their views on the aims of teacher training?

Some suggestions:

Set aside staff development time for discussion

It is important that all staff are given time to express their views on the participation of the school in a partnership scheme. There should be an opportunity for questions to be raised, for issues to be clarified and for anxieties to be expressed. But staff should also consider the professional characteristics, skills and knowledge required by an effective teacher and the contribution the school could make to the development of these. It is important that, ultimately, the staff as a group share a 'vision' of the aims of initial teacher training and so give students consistent guidance.

Consider the model of the teacher which is the basis of the HEI course

It is important for students that there is also agreement between the school and the HEI on the nature of good teaching and the aims of teacher education. If the views of the HEI on these matters are not clear in its documentation, then a meeting should be arranged with the HEI at which these issues are discussed.

(B): REVIEWING YOUR SCHOOL AS A CONTEXT FOR STUDENT LEARNING

In preparation for partnership, it may be helpful to undertake a review of the school's existing strengths and weaknesses as a context for students'

5

school-based learning. This review can then form the basis for development work and for INSET plans.

How can the strengths and weaknesses of your school as a place for training students be assessed?

Some suggestions:

Review the ethos of the school

It is crucial that the school environment in general is supportive of students. This means that it is best if all staff, whether or not they are directly involved in the student programme, are committed to it in principle. In order that the school can provide students with the best opportunities for professional growth, the following can be reviewed:

- the quality of teaching and learning;
- school policies and schemes of work;
- continuity of staffing;
- the balance of experienced and newly qualified staff;
- the experience of staff in working collaboratively;
- the readiness of staff to undertake INSET;
- the willingness of staff to engage in critical evaluation of their practice;
- the willingness of staff to make their classes available to students;
- the enthusiasm of staff to take on a more active mentoring role;
- the enthusiasm of the governing body to become involved in initial teacher training.

Consider your INSET needs

Schools will need to consider their INSET needs in relation to mentor training. Ways of meeting these needs might be to:

- request that the HEI make some specific provision;
- utilize external courses – most HEIs now offer award bearing and non-award bearing mentor training courses;
- arrange a programme of INSET to allow those who already possess appropriate skills or expertize to share these with colleagues;
- arrange a programme of in-house INSET by buying in consultants.

Assess the physical resources

Although space is at a premium in most schools, students' personal requirements will need to be taken into account. These include:

- space for their belongings;
- access to the staff room and to tea/coffee making facilities;
- somewhere quiet and private for discussions with their mentor.

Review liaison with the HEI

If partnerships are to be successful, close working relationships between schools and HEIs are essential. This means that the school should:

- review the existing channels of communication with the HEI;
- identify a school representative to liaise with the HEI. (This may or may not be the person eventually appointed to take on the role of senior mentor – see Section 1:4 'Appointing a senior mentor'.)

(C): ESTABLISHING PARTNERSHIP

It is likely that schools and HEIs will develop partnership in three areas:

- in promoting student learning;
- in the assessment of student teachers; and
- in the planning and administration of the course.

When establishing a partnership it may be useful to set up a steering group consisting of representatives from the school and the HEI. A key role of the steering group will be to draw up a 'contract' that specifies the roles, rights and responsibilities of both partners in the training processes. It may also specify the entitlement of student teachers. The following points may form the basis of discussion for the content of such a contract.

Partnership for student learning

Schools and HEIs may make different contributions to students' professional preparation, but these contributions are equally valuable; equally relevant; and equally necessary. The challenge in building an effective training programme is to integrate these different contributions and to use the knowledge, understandings and skills of both teachers and tutors as fully as possible.

What opportunities can be provided for colleagues to explore the different contributions of the school and the HEI to the training of student teachers?

Some suggestions:

Become familiar with the current curriculum of training

It is important that staff have an overview of the complete course of professional preparation that students currently receive. This information should be available from the HEI. Take particular note of:

- the different components of the course;
- the aims and outline content of each component;
- the times and nature of students' school experiences;
- the aims of each school experience.

Discuss the course documentation

Discussion on the course documentation will show where the school and the HEI can each contribute most significantly to student training. There will be aspects of the course where students will benefit from the perspectives of tutors and classroom teachers. Developing students' understanding of the teaching of the core curriculum is one such area (see Part B of this handbook). Students may also benefit from teachers leading school-based seminars on, for example, issues included in the HEIs *Educational and Professional Studies* programme (See Section 2.3). As this is an extremely complex issue staff should be given time to consider the course documentation and identify aspects of students' training to which they feel they could make a worthwhile contribution *before* meeting with the partner HEI.

Consider the use of partnership 'language'

It is important when establishing partnership arrangements with the HEI to ensure that you not only share a common vision of the aims of teacher training and of effective teaching but that you 'interpret' partnership language in the same way. For example, discussing what is meant by the term 'mentor' and how mentoring differs from the supervision of students, can help to clarify expectations.

Partnership in student assessment

Teachers will be in a strong position to make a significant contribution to the assessment of students' practical teaching competence (see Section 4).

You will need to clarify whether there is an expectation that you will formally assess students' competence on a regular basis and how many assessments the HEI intends to make. Will the HEI provide extra support in the case of a difficult or failing student? (see Section 4:3)

Partnership in planning and administration

If schools are to be involved in the management of a partnership scheme then it is important that they are fully aware of exactly what this means for them. As part of the partnership scheme many schools are being invited to participate in course planning. You will need, therefore, to consider the nature and degree of any contribution you might make to this aspect of initial teacher training. In addition, you will need to discuss as a whole staff the scope and degree of your involvement in, for example, reviewing students' school experience files and dealing with failing students. Clearly documented procedures will need to be developed to improve the efficiency and effectiveness of administration.

1.3:   Managing the scheme in your school

Mentoring student teachers makes considerable demands on the school as a whole. The scheme will therefore need careful management.

HOW CAN SUCH A SCHEME BE MANAGED EFFECTIVELY?

Some suggestions:

Appoint a member of staff to act as a senior mentor within the school

If a partnership scheme is to be effectively managed, then an established member of staff needs to be appointed to take on responsibility for students' school-based development. The responsibilities of the senior mentor are discussed in more detail in Section 1.4.

Establish a mentoring routine

However valuable informal contacts are, they are not in themselves sufficient as a way of supporting students' professional development; it is important that mentors establish a formal, weekly routine of work with students.

   The precise nature of the routine will depend on the school's agreed involvement in the scheme and the particular learning needs of the students. Nevertheless, it is suggested that within any contract drawn up between HEIs and their partner schools, mentors are allowed 'protected time' for formal discussion, planning and feedback with students. These formal mentoring sessions should take place in private (not in the staff room!) and should be recognized by the school as 'teaching time'. It is vitally important that mentors maintain a formal mentoring time even if they are informally talking to students about their work on other occasions during the week.

Establish a high profile for the scheme within the school as a whole

All members of staff within the school, whether or not they are directly involved with students on a day-to-day basis, need to be fully aware of the scheme and what is involved. This can be achieved by ensuring that:

- the details of the scheme are made known to all staff;
- all staff know the names of any students in the school, the courses that they are taking and the stage of their training;
- the issue of mentoring and student teachers is included as a routine item on all staff meeting agendas.

Mentors frequently comment that partnerships are *only* successful if the headteacher sees the training of student teachers as important and makes it a priority within the school!

Keep governors and parents fully informed

Governors will have been involved in the school's initial decision to accept students for training and in any necessary financial arrangements. However, they may still have concerns that need to be identified and addressed. They may, for example, be more aware of the demands of partnership and less aware of the benefits, such as staff development and additional resourcing. Again, the routine inclusion of the partnership scheme on the agenda for governors' meetings can do much to facilitate support.

Parents need to be informed too. A common concern is that pupils' work will suffer as a result of frequently being taught by student teachers. Careful explanation of the detailed working of the scheme, and especially of the role of collaborative teaching (see Section 2.6) can do much to reduce parents' worries. The routine reference to the scheme within the school prospectus, newsletters and the annual governors' report can also help to reassure concerned parents.

1.4: Appointing a senior mentor

As the involvement of schools in ITT has increased many headteachers have chosen to appoint a designated senior mentor. This person, usually an experienced teacher with some managerial responsibility, is given the task of planning and co-ordinating students teachers' work within the school. As the quality of the mentoring scheme will depend to a significant degree on the quality of the senior mentor, careful consideration needs to be given to this appointment. It is particularly important to clarify the responsibilities of the senior mentor by drawing up and circulating a 'job description' for this role.

WHAT MIGHT THE ROLE OF THE SENIOR MENTOR BE?

The exact role of the senior mentor is likely to vary from scheme to scheme. In some schools the senior mentor will take on a supportive and facilitative role. In others the senior mentor will be more interventionist, both in working with students and with colleagues. In general, however, managing the scheme within the school may involve the senior mentor in:

- inducting students into the school;
- assigning students to particular classes;
- running school-based seminars;
- observing students formally and providing them with feedback;
- monitoring and evaluating students' performance and keeping records according to agreed procedures;
- completing student assessment requirements;
- supporting class mentors in their work with students;
- responding to the INSET needs of class mentors;
- co-ordinating the work of subject mentors ;
- monitoring and evaluating the quality of the mentoring scheme overall;
- reporting to staff meetings;
- liaising with the HEI tutor.

WHAT TYPE OF PERSON WOULD FIT THE ROLE OF SENIOR MENTOR?

There are several characteristics it is important to consider:

Status

The senior mentor will need to advise and support colleagues in their work with students and it may therefore be appropriate that the teacher

11

appointed to this role has some status within the school. In many schools, the deputy head would be an appropriate choice for senior mentor, although another experienced and well-respected member of staff might be equally acceptable.

Professional practice

The senior mentor should be a good role model for student teachers. This means that the person appointed to this role should not only be a skilled practitioner but also someone who is open-minded and committed to developing her/his professional knowledge and skills.

Personal qualities

It is important that the senior mentor is able to deal sensitively with adult learners and with teacher colleagues, at both professional and personal levels. But the role of senior mentor makes other demands in terms of personal qualities. At the beginning of their school experience many students believe that the best way to learn to teach is through trial and error; essentially, they want to be left alone in their classrooms to make their own mistakes! Consequently students do not always appreciate the benefits of involvement in other forms of learning. It is for this reason that the senior mentor should be willing to *insist* that students carry out certain school-based tasks, attend seminars, visit other classes etc.

1.5:   Selecting class mentors

In many partnership arrangements a number of students will be on placement in any one school. Teachers other than the designated senior mentor will therefore necessarily be involved in the mentoring process.

WHAT SHOULD THE ROLE OF THE CLASS MENTOR BE?

As stated earlier, the involvement of schools in the professional preparation of student teachers will vary. It may be useful for schools to clarify the contribution of class mentors to each of the following:

- inducting students into the classroom;
- managing and overseeing students' work in the classroom;
- helping students to benefit from classroom observation;
- observing students and providing feedback;
- engaging in collaborative planning and teaching with students;
- student assessment.

Once the role of the class mentor has been more clearly defined, it should be circulated within the school.

WHICH TEACHERS SHOULD BECOME CLASS MENTORS?

In deciding which teachers should become class mentors it is important that both the needs of the pupils and the appropriateness of individual teachers to take on this role are taken into account.

- *The needs of the pupils.*

The needs of the pupils will obviously be a high priority in making this decision. It may be considered inappropriate to assign student teachers to particular classes or year groups. There may be debate, for example, as to whether students should be placed with pupils undertaking Standard Assessment Tasks.

- *The appropriateness of teachers.*

Student teachers often see the class mentor as the most significant person in their school-based learning. In the past, teachers were assigned students for a variety of reasons and the best interests of the student were not always taken into account. If schools are to take a key role in students' initial teacher training then it is crucial that the *appropriateness* of teachers who take on the role of class mentors is also carefully considered. The following questions might be useful in determining the suitability of teachers to take on this role:

- Would they provide a good role model for a student?
- Would they be prepared to develop their mentoring practice – learn how best to share their professional expertize and develop students' own knowledge and skill?
- Would they be willing to share their class with students?
- Would they deal sensitively with adult learners?
- Would they be prepared to accept students as individuals who bring with them a range of experiences and who need to find their *own* teaching styles?

NB The role of the subject mentor is rather different. It will therefore be addressed in Section 5 of this handbook.

1.6: Assessing and managing resources

Becoming a 'partner' in the professional preparation of teachers will inevitably make demands on schools in terms of resources. Before joining a partnership scheme headteachers will need to have a realistic understanding of the resource demands as well as the benefits of participation. They will also need to establish clear procedures for the resource management of the scheme as they will be accountable to the HEI and to OFSTED/OHMCI for their use.

HOW CAN THE RESOURCE DEMANDS OF THE SCHEME BE FAIRLY ASSESSED AND MANAGED?

Some suggestions:

Undertake an audit of the resource demands of the scheme

What is it important to consider?

Staff time –

The most important resource demand of mentoring is staff time. The amount of time required for mentoring will inevitably depend on the range and scope of the school's participation in the scheme, the number of students etc. To give an approximate guide, however, the senior mentor will need to be allocated a minimum of 45–60 minutes 'protected time' each week for: working with the student teacher; supporting and advising colleagues; liaising with the HEI tutor; and undertaking required administrative duties. This cost can obviously be reduced if there is more than one student on placement in the school.

Class mentors will spend considerable time working with students in informal ways – observing, planning, and discussing their teaching. Because this work is informal it is less easy to quantify. Nevertheless, it needs to be recognized as a legitimate demand on teachers' time. In addition, if partnership arrangements involve subject mentoring and the provision of school-based seminars, then these too have to accounted for.

Other costs –

Students will inevitably make demands on other school resources as well: materials, telephone, photocopying etc. These costs can be relatively easily assessed and guidelines need to be drawn up and clearly communicated to all staff, students teachers and the HEI.

Consider the potential benefits of partnership

When assessing the resource demands of the scheme it is necessary to balance these against the potential benefits of partnership for your school. There are three important areas where schools are likely to benefit from partnership: students as an additional staff resource; continuous professional development of staff; and job 'satisfaction'.

Students as an additional staff resource –

Even in the early stages of school experience, when students are more likely to be engaged in forms of collaborative teaching, pupils will clearly benefit from having an additional adult working in the classroom. At a later stage, when students are able to take greater responsibility for a class, these benefits can be considerable.

Professional development –

Taking responsibility for the systematic preparation of a new member of the profession is inevitably a powerful form of professional development in that:

- taking part in a well-organized partnership scheme brings colleagues into close working relationships with those in other schools and in higher education institutions;
- effective mentoring requires teachers to 'open doors' to colleagues;
- mentoring student teachers demands that teachers share and justify their own professional practice;
- many HEIs are offering their partner schools in-service training and award bearing courses on favourable terms.

Some commentators have argued that taking part in initial teacher education is the single most significant initiative that a school can take in supporting the professional development of its staff. As a result, it can be argued that some of the 'costs' of participating in school-based training should be seen as a legitimate charge on their INSET budget.

Job satisfaction –

Involvement in the initial training of teachers can give teachers an enhanced sense of job satisfaction. Involvement in ITT enables schools to exert a greater influence on shaping the next generation of teachers. Some mentors have commented that they see this as an opportunity to put something back into the profession. There is also a sense of satisfaction to be gained through observing individual students developing in confidence, knowledge and skill.

15

NB The particular benefits of subject mentoring in the primary school will be discussed in part B of this handbook.

Decide how resources are to be assigned

However the costs and benefits are assessed, when finances are transferred from the HEI to the school, headteachers will have to make decisions about how these are to be assigned. Schools are accountable for the appropriate use of these funds within the school. At least three possible strategies for the distribution of funds are possible and the advantages and disadvantages of each will have to be considered:

- direct payments to the senior mentor and other teachers involved (additional points on the pay scale);
- additional resources to the teachers involved;
- additional funding for the central staffing budget.

This last strategy does appear to allow the greatest flexibility. If HEIs can be encouraged to enter into firm agreements with schools well in advance, additional costs can be built into the central staffing budget. In this way mentors can be allocated regular non-contact time to work with student teachers. If supply cover is necessary, such an arrangement also allows the school to enter into long term rather than *ad hoc* arrangements with supply teachers.

1.7: Monitoring and evaluation

While the designated senior mentor will have the overall responsibility for planning a programme of student learning in the school, the contribution made by individual class mentors and other colleagues will be of fundamental significance. It is important that all contributions are recognized and acknowledged. Class mentors are likely to need continuous support from the senior mentor and possibly from curriculum co-ordinators. These colleagues may welcome opportunities to discuss ways in which they could develop their role and the prospects for further training. The effectiveness of their performance will also need to be evaluated.

HOW CAN THE QUALITY OF MENTORING BE MONITORED?

Some suggestions:

Ensure mentoring is given a high profile within the school

By agreeing to become a partner in initial teacher training you are committing your school to providing an appropriate and effective programme of development for each student teacher. Students have an entitlement to a well structured and supportive school experience. Mentors have an entitlement to the time and training that will enable them to be effective in their work with students. This will not happen if mentors are expected to debrief students during their morning break, or have their allocated mentoring time 'cut' to teach absent colleagues' classes.

Establish mechanisms for student feedback

The views of students should be built into the regular evaluation of the programme. These can be obtained through both informal discussion and more formal questionnaires. If they have not already done so, the HEI should, in collaboration with its partner schools, develop a common questionnaire to allow all schools to review the students' experience.

Include mentoring within staff appraisal

As an important part of the teacher's professional role, mentoring should be built into the school's regular appraisal procedures.

Encourage self-evaluation

Mentors should be encouraged to keep a record of their work with students. They should be encouraged to reflect critically on both the quality of their mentoring and on the model of good practice that they present to students.

Encourage mutual learning support

The task of mentoring can be stimulating and interesting. It can also be demanding. Mentors are likely to benefit from sharing their experiences with others both inside and outside the school. This is particularly important in small schools. Many partnership schemes are setting up support networks to link mentors working in different partnership schools. Good mentoring practice can be shared through newsletters and conferences.

THE ROLE OF THE HEI

HEI staff have the advantage of being familiar with a range of schools; they will therefore be an important resource in assisting with informal internal monitoring. In addition, the HEI should be encouraged to organize regular meetings for all their 'partner' schools so that different interpretations of the mentoring role, ways of organizing mentoring and the benefits and challenges of mentoring in different contexts can be discussed and evaluated.

Section 2

The Process of Mentoring

In this section we focus on the strategies, or tools, that are available for use by mentors (senior mentors, class mentors and subject mentors) in working with student teachers. Learning more about the process of mentoring is important for all those who work with students and we suggest that this and subsequent sections of this handbook are read widely within the school or used as the basis for INSET work.

Although we have set out the 'processes' of mentoring in a separate section, we do not see them as standing alone. Central to our view of mentoring is the idea that the way in which mentors and others use these strategies needs to change and develop in line with the learning needs of students. For example, the strategies used by mentors when working with students on their initial school experience will need to be very different from the strategies they will use when working with students who are on their final block teaching experience.

This section, which sets out the general principles underlying key mentoring strategies, should therefore be read in conjunction with Section 3 where we look in detail at the learning needs of students at different stages of their development and suggest ways in which teachers might use the strategies available to them in order to respond to students' learning needs.

2.1: Planning and preparation

Mentoring new entrants to the profession needs careful planning and preparation. It also means establishing a regular routine for working with students. But even before the students arrive, it is necessary to prepare for them.

WHAT PREPARATION SHOULD BE UNDERTAKEN BEFORE THE ARRIVAL OF STUDENTS?

Plan the students' time in school

It is wise to establish clear guidelines as to what proportion of their time students should spend:

- teaching;
- observing;
- undertaking structured activities;
- working on assignments;
- visiting other classes;
- attending school-based seminars.

How much time should be spent on each of these different activities will probably be discussed at the partnership steering group meetings. Much will depend on the learning needs of individual students and the nature of other demands being made on them by the HEI.

Plan where students are to be placed

In planning where students should be placed, careful consideration will need to be given to the learning needs of individual students and the particular expertize and teaching styles of class mentors. Consideration should also be given to the personalities of students and class mentors. For example, an 'outgoing' student may feel uncomfortable working with a quiet teacher (and vice versa), while placing a quiet student with an equally reserved class mentor may result in a total lack of communication! Where possible, it may be preferable to postpone decisions about the placement of students until they have made several preliminary visits to the school.

Working with other teachers

While working in a sustained way with a single class is an essential element in all primary teachers' preparation, there are advantages in exposing students, even for quite short periods of time, to a variety of different classes. This is particularly the case in the early stages of students' training. If students are to work with more than one teacher, it will be necessary to:

- think carefully about which other teachers and classes should be involved. It may be beneficial for students to visit different age groups, key stages or teachers with contrasting teaching styles;

- make clear to the teachers involved what is expected of students at this stage of their training and how they might work with the students;

Prepare a school development record

It will be necessary for a record to be kept of each student's experiences, progress and attainment in school. This should include information such as the student's curriculum vitae (see 2.2), details of the induction programme, teaching placements, visits to other classes, school-based tasks undertaken and seminars attended (see below), records of all formal meetings, completed observation schedules, profile review forms and action plans (see Section 4).

Plan the ways in which students might be integrated into the staff

A great deal of students' school-based learning will come about through their informal contact with staff. If they are to benefit fully from this informal learning, it is essential that they become integrated into the life of the staff room and the school.

Students need to have the opportunity to discuss their teaching with a wide range of colleagues as often as possible – over coffee, on playground duty, after school etc. It is the job of the senior mentor to make sure that students are integrated into the staff in a way that will allow this informal learning to take place.

The senior mentor should also consider whether there are any particular members of staff of a similar age and background that the student might benefit from getting to know well – students often indicate that they value informal contact with newly qualified teachers.

Decide how you will introduce students to the pupils

A decision on this should be made before the students arrive at the school. Should it be made clear, for example, that they are 'students'? There are both advantages and disadvantages in doing this. What is needed is a clear policy that is followed throughout the school.

Draw up an induction timetable for the students

You will also need to plan an induction programme for students. This should be presented to students on arrival. What might be included in an induction programme is addressed in 2.2 below.

Plan a programme of school-based seminars

As part of partnership schemes, many schools are becoming involved in running school-based seminars. The number of seminars run by schools and any transfer of funds that might be made for undertaking this work should be part of early partnership negotiations (See Section 1.6, *Assessing and Managing Resources*). The particular concern here is with planning an appropriate programme of school-based seminars.

There are three main reasons why these seminars are an appropriate and effective way of managing students' learning:

- there are key areas of difficulty, concern and interest that appear to be common to many students at particular stages of their school experience;
- there are important educational issues that can be effectively explored by students working in the school context;
- over time teachers will have developed a great deal of practical expertize. This can usefully be shared with groups of students working together in school.

These factors are of significance when planning a programme of school-based seminars. In deciding on the content of these seminars, schools and HEIs might consider:

Students' developmental needs –

Students appear to have many common difficulties and concerns at particular stages of their development. Classroom control, for example, is often a major concern in the early stages of students' school experience, while at a later stage, students might usefully focus on issues such as differentiation or assessment.

Students' college-based studies –

If it is decided that certain seminars will explore issues addressed as part of the *Educational and Professional Studies* component of the course, then schools should ask for a copy of the current programme and an outline of key points made and issues raised in relation to each topic. If seminars are to involve subject-specific work then schools will also need to know something of the content of students' subject studies.

The particular learning experiences the school can offer –

Teachers are ideally placed to develop students' professional understandings in a *real*, practical context. Teachers can effectively work with groups of students and examine, for example, long, medium and short term planning in their school, how they manage and organize the teaching of reading, the use they make of mathematics schemes and the like. There may also be features and factors significant to individual schools that could provide a focus for seminars: bilingualism, for example or the challenges and benefits of working in a small school.

2.2: Induction of student teachers

Student teachers need inducting into the school as a whole and into the classes in which they will be working. Inducting students into the school as a whole will be the responsibility of the senior mentor although some headteachers may wish to be involved in this process.

WHAT NEEDS TO BE INCLUDED IN AN EFFECTIVE 'WHOLE SCHOOL' INDUCTION PROGRAMME?

Suggestions of the possible items that might be included in a *whole school* induction programme are listed below. Individual schools will wish to decide what items they will select from this list and how they might add to it.

Welcoming students

Ensure an appropriate member of staff will be available to meet and welcome students on their first day.

Obtain details of students' previous experience

Students may be asked to provide schools with a curriculum vitae which outlines not only their previous school experience but in addition, any information which may be significant to their placement – subject specialisms, other qualifications, work experience, leisure interests etc.

Give students an induction timetable

This should outline the induction programme prepared for students – dates and times as well as purposes of any visits/meetings arranged, details of tasks to be undertaken etc.

Give students key documentation

This may include:

- the school prospectus;
- policy documents – including child protection guidelines and policies which address issues such as equal opportunities and bullying;
- the programme of school-based seminars.

Introduce key people

- headteacher;
- deputy head;
- school secretary;
- caretaker.

Show students key places

- staff room;
- lavatories;
- office;
- rooms designated for particular purposes/curriculum areas;
- school library.

Establish the school's expectations of all students while they are in school

- standards of dress;
- times of attendance;
- procedures for notifying absence;
- use of staff room (explain 'rules' concerning tea/coffee making facilities);
- use of photocopier;
- use of resources;
- access to meetings, INSET events;
- attendance of school-based seminars;
- relationship with support staff and parents;
- confidentiality;
- extra-curricular activities.

Explain school organization and procedures

- times of the school day;
- disciplinary codes and procedures;
- school assemblies;
- special needs provision;
- arrangements for first aid;
- safety procedures.

Clarify what records you want students to keep

Most student teachers are expected to keep a school experience file that records their medium-term and short-term planning, individual lesson plans, lesson evaluations and so on. Ensure that students – and class mentors – are aware of the purpose of this file and who has access to it.

Schools may also ask students who are undertaking an extended teaching experience to keep a portfolio of 'evidence', collected from various sources, of their developing competence, understanding and identity as a teacher. Students may choose to include in the portfolio particular and significant lesson evaluations, teaching materials, photographs, children's work, observation schedules, self-assessment schedules and the like.

Involvement in more active forms of learning

In the early stages of students' school experience, there is necessarily a great deal of information to convey. There will be some occasions on which it is necessary simply to impart information, but it is also vitally important to provide students with opportunities to ask questions and discuss what they have observed, both among themselves (if there is more than one student in the school), and with key members of staff. A good induction programme might also involve students in undertaking a number of school-based tasks.

WHAT STUDENT 'TASKS' ARE APPROPRIATE FOR INCLUSION IN A WHOLE SCHOOL INDUCTION PROGRAMME?

Activities 6.1 and 6.2 in Part B of this handbook could be used as part of students' induction into the whole school. In addition, students could explore the following:

School routines and rituals

Students could be asked to make note of the school routines and rituals. For example, what happens to the pupils during break time and lunch time? On what occasions do pupils meet as a school/key stage/ year group? Are there certain curricular activities that are taught by subject specialists? How is this organized?

Special needs support

The students could spend some time working alongside the special educational needs co-ordinator (SENCO) or, where appropriate, visit a unit attached to the school for children with particular learning difficulties.

Nursery provision

Where there is nursery provision, students may benefit from visiting the nursery class and exploring the curriculum, routines, resources and the like.

Local area

Students could be asked to carry out a brief survey of the local area, noting 'resources' – i.e. factories, shops, churches, parks, waste ground etc., that could enhance and provide a focus for pupils' learning. (NB: Not everything needs to happen on the first day students arrive. If students are to work in your school for some time, some aspects of induction might be best spread over several weeks.)

While senior mentors will be responsible for inducting students into the school, it is class mentors who will induct students into their individual classrooms.

WHAT NEEDS TO BE INCLUDED IN AN EFFECTIVE CLASSROOM INDUCTION PROGRAMME?

Below are listed some of the possible items that might be included in a 'classroom' induction programme. It is up to individual class mentors to decide what items they would add to this list and what they would leave out.

Introduce key people

- other teaching colleagues, including support teachers;
- the nursery nurse;
- parent helpers.

Provide appropriate documentation

- relevant long-term and medium-term plans – in particular, for the core curriculum areas;
- schemes of work;
- timetable for use of shared areas/rooms;
- rota for playground duty.

Describe/demonstrate resources

- teaching materials;
- resources for different classroom activities;
- classroom library;
- information technology.

Outline classroom organization and procedures

- safety procedures;
- routines for the beginning and end of the day (see suggested activity – 'Classroom routines and rituals' below);
- routines for moving the children from one part of the school to another, e.g. hall to the playground;
- routines for children visiting the lavatory;
- disciplinary procedures including support available;
- special needs support.

WHAT STUDENT TASKS ARE APPROPRIATE FOR A CLASSROOM INDUCTION PROGRAMME?

The activities described in Section 6 of this handbook could be used as part of students' induction into the classroom. In addition, students could explore the following:

Classroom routines and rituals

Students could make note of what pupils are expected to do:

- when they come into the classroom first thing in the morning;
- before and after their morning break/lunch time; and
- at the end of the day.

They could also note other classroom routines and rituals, for example:

- how the register is marked;

- how dinner money/bank etc. is organized; and
- who distributes and clears away resources.

The physical context

Students could examine the layout of the classroom – the positioning of tables, subject-specific resources, sinks etc. Where appropriate students could consider how teachers manage the use of shared space or open plan teaching situations.

NB: The same principles apply to classroom induction as to school induction. Pace your induction – students do not need to cover everything on the first day. Try to devise activities for students so that they can find some things out for themselves rather than being told everything. Recognize that students will inevitably need to return to all of the issues covered in the induction during the weeks that follow.

2.3: Running school-based seminars

We have suggested that it is the senior mentor who is likely to take on responsibility for running school-based seminars. In addition, in Section 2.1 we outlined a number of issues that might be considered when drawing up a programme of seminars. The focus here is on how to manage and organize a seminar effectively.

HOW CAN SENIOR MENTORS MANAGE AND STRUCTURE EFFECTIVE SCHOOL-BASED SEMINARS?

Some suggestions:

Set the ground rules

Make it clear to students at the start of the programme of seminars what can and cannot be discussed. Are students allowed to refer to negative aspects of colleagues' practice? Is there to be a rule of confidentiality about comments made within seminar discussions?

Plan the seminar in advance

As in any teaching situation, if seminars are to be effective then they need to be thoroughly planned. Ensure that you consider the specific purpose of the seminar, how it is to be structured and what resources you will need.

Ask students to prepare for the seminar

On occasions it may be useful to ask students to carry out certain tasks in preparation for the seminar – for example:

- observations;
- teaching activities;
- audit of resources,

and to bring notes of their observations, explorations etc. with them.

Involving colleagues

While senior mentors will take responsibility for running the seminar programme, it is often appropriate to involve a number of other colleagues. For example, the SENCO, curriculum co-ordinators and parent helpers could all make valuable contributions to the seminar programme. Ensure that all contributors are clear about the aims of the seminar programme and expectations in terms of their input.

Use a variety of teaching and learning strategies

Consider, in relation to the focus and purpose of each seminar, the appropriateness of different teaching/learning strategies. As in your work with pupils, there will be a place for explanation, demonstration, questioning etc. Do not structure all seminars in the same way: as well as whole group discussions consider presentations (individual or collaborative), 'brainstorming' sessions, practical workshop activities etc.

Keep the seminar 'on track'

Do not let seminars become dominated by any one group member. Ensure all students are encouraged to participate. In addition, do not let seminars be hijacked by students complaining about how tired they are, about difficult pupils etc. This is not the most productive use of seminar time. If necessary, allocate a specific and limited time in each seminar for 'moans and groans'. Be supportive and try to draw out important issues underlying students' complaints, such as the demands of primary teaching and the possible reasons for pupils' disruptive behaviour.

Recognize students' previous experiences

Adult learners will have a whole range of different life experiences, qualifications and talents. Some student teachers will have held demanding and high status posts in industry, commerce and the like. Try to ensure these experiences are recognized and used to their full advantage.

Figure 2.1: A school-based seminar discussion group

2.4:   Helping students to observe

Observing an experienced practitioner is one of the most important strategies for learning any complex activity. It is for this reason that, for many years, student teachers have been introduced to teaching by spending some part of their teaching practice sitting at the back of the classroom observing experienced teachers. But observation is not as straightforward as it seems. If it is going to be a productive learning experience, observation has to be carefully planned and followed up afterwards in discussion with the mentor.

HOW CAN MENTORS AND CLASS TEACHERS ENSURE THAT STUDENTS BENEFIT FROM THEIR PERIODS OF OBSERVATION?

Some suggestions:

Observing teachers

One of the difficulties students face when first observing experienced teachers is that they often find it very difficult to know what to observe. Teaching is such a complex activity that a naive observer may either see teaching as straightforward or else be overwhelmed by its complexity. If students are to get the most out of their periods of observation, they need to be given a clear focus for their work. The focus of students' observations will vary greatly, depending on the individual needs of students and their stage of development.

In the early stages of learning to teach, students might observe the routines, rules and rituals of classroom practice: for example, lesson beginnings and conclusions; strategies to gain the attention of the whole class; what pupils are required to do when they have finished set tasks (see also Section 3.1).

This could be followed by observation of specific teaching strategies and techniques: students could carefully observe class mentors instructing, explaining, questioning etc. (see Section 3.2). There are several activities in Sections 7, 8 and 9 that are appropriate for this purpose (see, for example, activities 7.1, 7.2, 7.6, 7.8 and 9.6).

At a later stage in their development, students might focus on pupils' learning and effective ways of teaching to support that learning (see Section 3.3). The activities described in Sections 7–9 would provide a useful structure for students' observations. In addition, several of the activities described in Sections 7–9 ask students to observe pupils working in the classroom: for example, activities 7.4, 7.5 and 8.3. Students might also find it helpful to use the 'pupil-focused observation schedule' referred to in Section 4 – *Student Assessment.*

Towards the end of their school experience, students might use observation for the specific aim of increasing the breadth and depth of their understanding of the process of teaching and learning. This may be achieved by, for example, observing how different teachers approach the teaching of a particular topic or concept (see Section 3.4).

Whatever the stage of students' development, it is vital that the focus of their observation is clearly specified. The quality and specificity of observation can be further helped if mentors:

Suggest ways in which students might collect evidence to support their observations

Collecting evidence further sharpens observation. Strategies might include asking students to:

- draw up simple observation schedules;
- talk to pupils about the activities they are undertaking – the purpose of the activity, what they have found out/learnt etc.;
- examine pupils' work.

Vary the activities that students undertake so that they are not always passive observers

Too much passive observation can be boring; a mixture of activities is therefore preferable. It is possible for students to have an observational focus in mind while at the same time taking some supportive role in the teaching process.

Ask students to report back on their observations either immediately afterwards or in their designated mentoring session

Discussing students' observations is valuable in that it helps students to *see* more clearly what they have observed while also allowing the mentor to monitor students' developing understanding of the teaching process. If, despite structuring their observations in this way, students still fail to appreciate the complexity of the issues they are considering, it may be necessary further to *sharpen* the focus of observation.

NB It is often the case that once students have developed basic teaching skills and are responsible for teaching the whole class, they are no longer given the time and opportunity to observe experienced teachers or pupils. Observation is an important strategy for students' learning *throughout* their training.

Figure 2.2: A 'non-passive' student observing a class

2.5: Observing students and giving feedback

One of the most valuable strategies that can be used in supporting students' development is regular planned observation and systematic feedback. Informal observation and feedback is vitally important if students are to benefit from their time in school. However, it is also valuable to establish a more formal observation and feedback routine. This routine needs to happen on a regular basis – if possible once a week – and needs to be planned just as carefully as any other 'teaching' activity.

Careful thought needs to be given as to who will be responsible for the formal observation and feedback – the senior mentor, or the class mentor. If this responsibility is taken on by the senior mentor, then she or he will need access to the classroom where the student is teaching; in some schools this may be appropriate, in others, it may not. If formal observation and feedback is to be undertaken by the class mentor then it will be essential to establish some means whereby the senior mentor is kept fully informed of each student's progress. Whoever is responsible, records should be kept of all formal meetings with students.

Once again, the detailed purpose and focus of observation and feedback will vary, depending on students' individual needs and their particular stage of development. In this section we aim to set out some of the general principles of this aspect of mentoring.

WHAT SHOULD MENTORS AND STUDENTS DO IN ORDER TO MAKE THE MOST OF OBSERVATION AND FEEDBACK?

The routine of observation and feedback involves three distinct activities:

- preliminary planning;
- undertaking observation; and
- giving feedback.

Some suggestions for preliminary planning:

Establish a clear focus for observation

When observing students, mentors inevitably find it necessary to consider a wide range of points that arise from the teaching itself. However, simply responding to *whatever emerges* is not enough. It is valuable also to decide in advance what the particular focus of the observation session is to be. This is likely to change as the student develops. For example, after the first week or so of their initial teaching experience, students may benefit from feedback on particular *teaching skills* – beginning and ending activities, the use of their voice, their questioning techniques. The list of criteria set out by the government (*see* pages 85–87) provides a useful preliminary framework here. At a later stage, observation might take a different focus – for example, providing feedback on pupils' responses to an activity.

Ensure that the student knows what the focus of observation is to be

As we suggest in Section 3, in the early stages of work with students, the focus for formal observation is perhaps best decided by mentors; later in their development students will benefit from selecting the focus for observation themselves. In this way it is possible for mentors progressively to encourage students to take responsibility for their own professional development. Whoever chooses the focus for formal observation, it is essential that both the mentor and student are fully aware of that focus before observation takes place.

NB As well as using the government criteria as a framework for observation there are several activities in Sections 7–9 that suggest a focus for mentors' observations of students' performance. These include English activities 7.1, 7.2, 7.6 and 7.8; mathematics activities 8.2, 8.4 and 8.8; and science activities 9.2 and 9.8.

Some suggestions for undertaking observation:

Frequency and duration

In the past, the frequency with which mentors have formally observed their students has varied considerably. We suggest that every student should be formally observed at least once a week. Such formal observation should take place even if the mentor is collaboratively teaching alongside the student on other occasions during the week, since the purposes of collaborative teaching are rather different from those of formal observation.

Role

During observation, mentors can adopt a variety of different roles, each of which may have advantages and disadvantages. These include:

- Quietly sitting at the back of the classroom. This approach leaves the mentor free to observe and collect evidence on the student's 'performance', but it may provide only limited access to the pupils' work.
- Actively participating in the lesson. The advantage of taking a more active role is that it can give greater insight into the planning and purposes behind the student's teaching. However, if the mentor becomes too involved in the teaching itself, it is inevitably more difficult to observe systematically.

Whatever role the mentor decides to adopt – and it may be a combination of the two outlined above – that role needs to be clearly explained to the student beforehand. Only in the most extreme circumstances (for example, in cases of danger or serious disruption) should the mentor *take over* the lesson from the student in an unplanned way.

Collecting evidence

Giving students verbal feedback on their teaching is valuable but not sufficient. It is also important to provide them with some evidence of what has been observed. As we will see in the next section, evidence can significantly help in the process of providing feedback to students. A number of strategies can be used including:

- Proformas/recording schedules – Many partnership schemes are developing a range of proformas that may be used for observation purposes (see, for example, the observation schedules included in Section 4). You may wish to develop these along with your partner HEI. Once again, the list of government criteria provides a good starting point.

- Notes – On some occasions and for some purposes mentors may consider proformas to be too formal or too restrictive. In these circumstances, hand-written notes are a useful alternative. These notes may take a number of forms. They may, for example, simply be a *stream of consciousness* – a record of the mentor's own judgements on the strengths and weaknesses of a particular aspect of the student's practice. Alternatively, they may include more *objective* evidence such as descriptions of pupils' responses to a student's instructions/questions etc. Alternative sources of evidence might include samples of pupils' work or audio or video recording.

The aim of systematic feedback is to help students develop a clearer understanding of their own teaching – both its strengths and its weaknesses. It is this understanding that enables students to bring their teaching more directly under their control. Providing students with appropriate feedback that achieves this aim is one of the most challenging skills of mentoring.

WHEN GIVING FEEDBACK, WHAT FACTORS SHOULD MENTORS CONSIDER?

Timing

Giving feedback to students immediately after a lesson is obviously valuable, but not always possible. Schedule observations so that they can be followed up reasonably quickly in the formal mentoring session. If it is not possible to follow up an observation immediately with your student, try to give at least some very brief feedback straight away. Even a short discussion will be appreciated by the student, provided it is clear that there will be an opportunity for a longer review at a later stage.

If immediate feedback is likely to be difficult on a number of occasions then an alternative strategy might be to ask the student to keep a journal in which you can write brief comments during the course of the lesson. This has the advantage of providing the student with at least some immediate feedback and can act as an aide-memoir for further discussion at a later stage.

Type of feedback

One particular difficulty in providing feedback is getting the right balance between negative and positive comments. If mentors are too critical they can undermine students' confidence. Alternatively mentors can *kill by kindness*. It is important to remember that, however confident they may appear, students are extremely vulnerable. Take care to plan the feedback – both the positive and the negative points that need to be made. However bad the lesson, try and find at least some good points to comment on – be constructive.

Prioritize the negative points that need to be made. If there are a number of weaknesses, do not cover everything at once. Stick to the agreed focus and one or two of the other most pressing difficulties. Allow students the opportunity to give their view of the lesson. Insist that they consider its strengths as well as its weaknesses. This can be a useful way of beginning a feedback session.

Style of feedback

There are a number of different styles of providing feedback to students, each of which has a different educational purpose. You need to have at your disposal a repertoire of styles that you can utilize in different circumstances, depending on what you identify as the key learning needs of the student. Any one feedback session might well involve a combination of different styles. Three principal styles can be simply described:

Didactic

This is where the mentor takes the lead, identifies the issues to be considered, interprets the evidence that has been collected and gives directive feedback to the student. This strategy is particularly appropriate when mentors are giving tightly focused advice on specific teaching strategies.

Discursive

This is where, through a series of directed questions and the presentation of evidence (observational evidence, examples of pupils' work), students are asked to identify and analyze specific aspects of their teaching. While this strategy is time-consuming it has a number of distinct advantages:

- It encourages students to analyze and interpret their teaching themselves while allowing mentors to maintain control of the *agenda* of issues to be addressed;
- It can be particularly valuable with weak students where a more direct approach might be seen as threatening;
- Skillful questioning by mentors can also enable students to appreciate the complexity of teaching: that there are no clear-cut solutions to the difficulties and dilemmas teachers face in the classroom.

Partnership

In this strategy the mentor encourages the student to take the lead in identifying the issues to be considered as well as in their interpretation. The mentor provides evidence, but both mentor and student together discuss the meaning of the evidence in a spirit of open professional enquiry.

This *partnership* model is particularly valuable in the later stages of student development where the aim is both to encourage students to take greater responsibility for their own professional development and to help them confront some of the complexities of the teacher's role. In reality, any one feedback session might well involve a combination of these different styles.

2.6: Collaborative teaching

One of the main challenges for developing more effective school-based learning is to find ways of giving students access to the wealth of practical knowledge that experienced teachers possess. To an inexperienced observer, teaching can seem a simple activity. It is only as they gain experience themselves that students come to appreciate some of the complexities involved. Yet, despite its complexity (or perhaps because of it), teachers often find it difficult to talk about their work in any detail to outsiders. One of the great strengths of collaborative teaching, where students and mentors plan and teach together, is that the student becomes an *insider* to the teaching process. As a result, collaborative teaching can become an important means for helping students gain access to their mentor's practical knowledge.

WHAT IS COLLABORATIVE TEACHING?

There are a great many ways of teaching collaboratively with students, ranging from situations where students teach only one small aspect of the lesson – for example, working with a particular group of pupils or explaining a particular concept – to full and equal joint teaching. Whatever the role assigned to students, an essential feature of collaborative teaching is that they are part of the planning process. Even if they are not taking responsibility for the whole lesson, students need to understand fully what it is that the teacher is trying to achieve and their own role within that process. Simply to give them a small group of pupils to work with on their own without involving them in the planning of the whole lesson is not adequate. Such a strategy may at first sight seem attractive, but if the result is to isolate the student from the teacher's thinking, it will prove an inadequate preparation for taking responsibility for teaching, managing and organizing the whole class.

WHAT ARE THE ADVANTAGES OF COLLABORATIVE TEACHING?

Collaborative teaching facilitates student learning in a number of way:

Modelling

By working jointly with teachers, students have the opportunity to model themselves on those teachers. Modelling is a vitally important source of learning for students, particularly in the early stages of learning to teach.

Access to teachers' knowledge

Through the process of joint planning, students gain access to the background knowledge on which teachers draw when planning their lessons. That knowledge, which is often complex and detailed, is largely implicit in teaching. Joint planning provides a vehicle by which teachers can help students gain access to this knowledge.

A non-threatening context for beginning teaching

In the early stages of learning to teach, collaborative teaching provides a safe and non-threatening context in which students can begin teaching.

A context for focusing on particular teaching strategies or skills

Students can focus on the development of particular skills in a carefully programmed way while the class teacher retains responsibility for the remainder of the lesson.

Collaborative teaching also facilitates pupil learning:

Pupils are less often exposed to unsupported student teaching

One of the concerns of parents and governors in the move to school-based teacher training is that pupils will spend too much time working with students. A well-structured programme of collaborative teaching is likely significantly to reduce this concern.

Two adults will be teaching in the same class

With two adults in the classroom there is more opportunity for differentiation of tasks and individual support.

WHO SHOULD BE INVOLVED IN COLLABORATIVE TEACHING?

The class mentor should obviously be the person most frequently involved in collaborative teaching with her/his student, but there are many advantages in students occasionally teaching collaboratively with the senior mentor and other teachers as well. If this is to be the case then those other teachers need to be fully briefed on what their role will be.

HOW MUCH COLLABORATIVE TEACHING SHOULD STUDENTS UNDERTAKE?

At the early stages of their school experience, there are obvious advantages in students spending a substantial proportion of their *teaching* time working collaboratively. As they gain in confidence, students should be given progressively more responsibility for the whole class. Collaborative teaching will influence student/pupil dynamics and mentors should gradually *step back* and allow students to take the leading role. However, there are advantages in maintaining some collaborative teaching throughout students' school experience. Collaborative teaching can be a useful strategy for supporting more advanced forms of professional development as well as supporting beginners.

WHAT ARE THE PROCEDURES OF COLLABORATIVE TEACHING?

Collaborative teaching involves three distinct processes: joint planning; joint teaching; and review.

Joint planning

As we have already noted, one of the key advantages of collaborative teaching is that through joint planning, students have the opportunity to gain detailed insight into the thinking and planning undertaken by an experienced teacher. Experienced teachers rarely plan in the same detail as student teachers. However, as a preparation for collaborative teaching, careful and explicit planning is essential. Although this process may be time consuming, making explicit the basis of their craft knowledge and expertize can be a powerful form of professional development for teachers.

What might mentors discuss with students when jointly planning a lesson?

Some suggestions :

- Discuss the purposes of the activity, emphasising the learning objectives;
- Clarify the introduction, development and conclusion of the activity and the rationale for particular methods of organization and teaching strategies to be used;
- Explore how the activity is to be made relevant and meaningful to pupils;
- Consider the selection, preparation and use of resources;
- Discuss how the work is to be differentiated to meet particular children's learning needs and identify assessment opportunities.

It is vitally important that you also:

- Identify those aspects of the teaching that the student is to undertake;
- Plan students' *contributions* with them in more detail;
- Clarify your responsibilities as class mentor within the lesson;
- Agree who is to take responsibility for the overall management and control of the class.

Joint teaching

There are many different ways of teaching collaboratively, involving different degrees of responsibility for students and different teaching strategies. Each should be carefully chosen to support students' learning needs at their particular stage of development.

At a general level, the range of a student's responsibility may vary on a continuum between mentor takes main responsibility, student assists; and student takes main responsibility, mentor assists. There are many permutations between these extremes. The range of specific teaching strategies is also extensive. Below are some suggestions:

- the student take responsibility for teaching one aspect of the lesson to the whole class: for example, the beginning or end of the lesson; the introduction of a key concept; a question and answer session;
- the student works with particular individuals or groups of pupils for part or all of the lesson: for example, listening to pupils read, taking responsibility for differentiated work with a particular group;
- The student and mentor make a joint presentation to the class, adopting different roles: for example, taking opposing sides in an argument, taking different *voices* in reading the class story.

Reviewing the teaching

Many of the principles described in relation to giving students feedback also apply to reviewing collaborative teaching. For example, timing is important. If at all possible, a review should be held soon after the collaborative teaching has taken place. In addition, the review session needs to be carefully planned in order to consider both the positive and negative aspects of a student's *performance*.

However, commenting on the student's *performance* is not the sole aim of this review. Because the teaching is jointly planned and executed, it is possible to deepen the student's understanding of the teaching process through a discussion of the mentor's own practice as well as the student's. Once again, the range of issues that might be addressed is extensive; the following are merely suggestions. For example, you might:

- return to the lesson plan and evaluate the appropriateness of the aims of the lesson and the teaching strategies used in the light of experience;
- discuss the way in which it was necessary to adapt the lesson plan in response to pupils' learning needs or unforeseen circumstances;

- discuss the quality of the children's learning and of the learning outcomes.

NB – Several activities described in Sections 6–9 of this handbook specifically suggest that the mentor becomes involved in some aspect of collaborative teaching. These include activities 6.6, 7.2 and 7.5. A fuller appreciation of how collaborative teaching may be used in supporting students at different stages of their development can be gained by reading the section entitled *The Stages of Mentoring*.

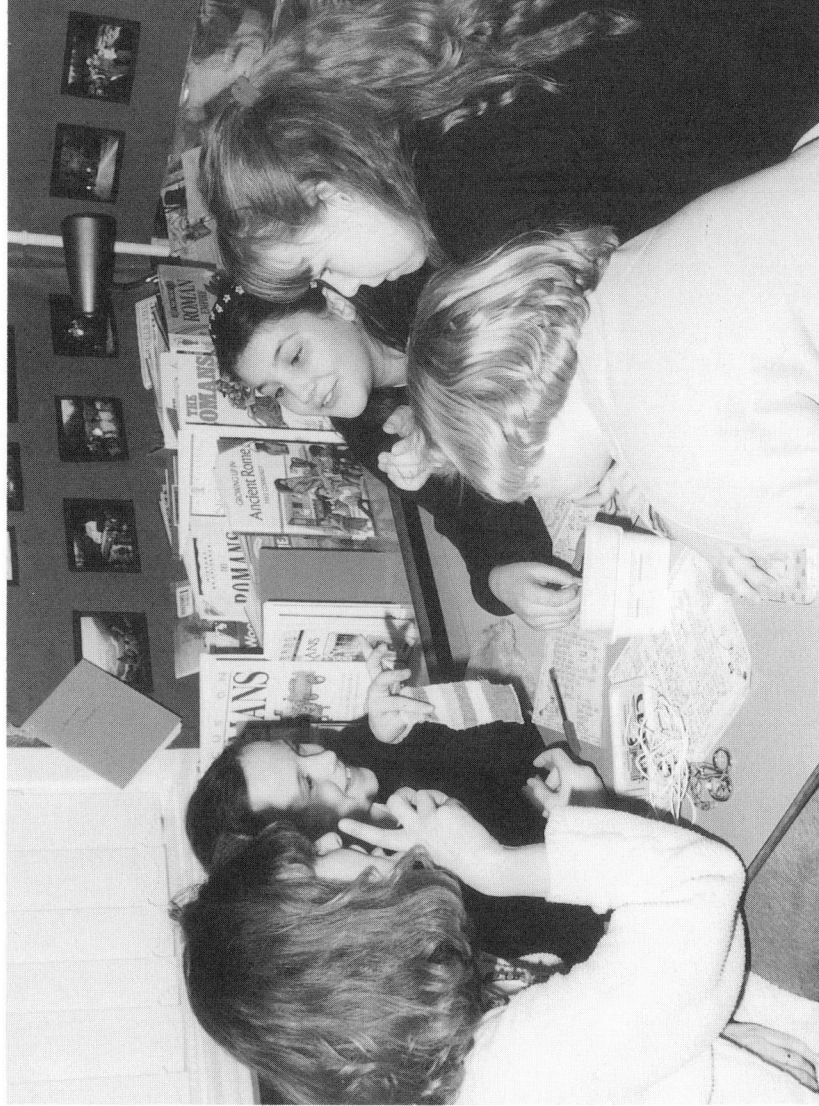

Figure 2.3: Student involved in collaborative teaching with a small group of pupils

Section 3

The Stages of Mentoring

Introduction

In recent years, a great deal of research has been carried out into how students learn to teach. One of the common findings of this research is that during the learning process, students typically go through a number of different stages of development.

Before they begin their training, it is not uncommon for student teachers to be highly idealistic about teaching. For many students, this involves wanting to identify closely with the pupils and with their needs and interests. This identification with the pupils is hardly surprising; for the vast majority of students in training, their only experience of the teaching process has been as pupils themselves. Once they enter the classroom, this idealism quickly fades!

The first days and weeks in the classroom are extremely challenging for students, both professionally and personally. One of the common complaints that students make in these early days is that they find it difficult to *see* – they find it difficult to disentangle the complexities of teaching and understand the processes involved. Either they assume that it is straightforward or they are overwhelmed by its complexity. Learning how to observe experienced teachers and understand the different skills that they are using is an achievement in itself; students need to be taught how to do this.

Another important feature of early classroom experience is that students frequently become obsessed with their own survival. Rather than wanting to identify closely with the pupils, they become dominated by their concern to manage them. Achieving class management and control becomes an overriding concern. Teaching and learning activities are judged almost entirely in terms of whether they contribute to achieving that end. Our own research has shown that students often find this early period of learning to teach highly stressful. Many find it hard to come to terms with themselves as an authority figure. They have to get used to a new persona – *me as teacher* – and for some, it is not a character they particularly like. As a consequence, it is not uncommon for students to go through a period of resenting the pupils for forcing them to be more authoritarian than they really want to be.

Eventually, most students do manage at least to *act* like a teacher; they learn how to control the class and engage the pupils in some purposeful activity. However, once students have achieved a basic level of competence, they may reach a plateau and stop developing. Many students appear to have found one way of teaching that *works* and are determined to stick to it! Some students even seem to lose their motivation and commitment. They may, for example, lower their expectations with regard to pupils' work and behaviour or begin to take short-cuts with their lesson planning. The challenge at this point is for mentors to move students on from *acting* like a teacher to *thinking* like a teacher. We suggest that one of the key differences between these two states is that experienced teachers are able to *decentre*: they are able to devote their attention to thinking about their pupils' learning and appropriate ways of teaching to support that learning, rather than simply focusing on their own performance. If students are to improve the quality of their teaching, it is essential that they too learn to *decentre*. Evidence suggests that, without external support, students often find this transition difficult.

There is one further stage of learning to teach and that involves the development of students as independent reflective practitioners. In recent years, critics have described the term reflective practitioner as a slogan in search of a definition. Certainly defining the term with any precision is difficult and, however it is defined, a course of initial professional preparation can do no more than lay the foundations for its development. Nevertheless, it is clear that, as they gain in confidence, students are capable of:

- taking more responsibility for their own professional development;
- broadening their repertoire of teaching strategies;
- deepening their understanding of the complexities of teaching and learning; and
- considering the social, moral and political dimensions of educational practice.

In the past, the development of these abilities and understandings has been seen as the sole responsibility of the HEI. We suggest that, although the contribution of those in higher education is essential, if these abilities and understandings are to be developed in a way that is meaningful to students, they will also need appropriate support from mentors.

It is because students typically go through these different stages of learning to teach that mentoring needs to be developmental too. However, it is important to emphasise that, in arguing for a developmental approach, we are not simply suggesting that mentors should give students the sort of support that they ask for. If students are to develop fully, then there will be times when mentors will need to be assertive in their interventions, providing students with what they perceive them to need rather than what the students want! However, in essence, mentoring is no different from any other form of teaching – it needs to start from where the learners are and take their typical pattern of development into account.

In this section of the handbook, we outline a number of different stages of mentoring. For each stage we identify different learning priorities for students and a different *role* for mentors in supporting those learning needs. We also suggest a number of key mentoring strategies, that are intended to be considered flexibly and with sensitivity. In fact, it is probably more appropriate to think of each stage as cumulative rather than discrete. As students develop, mentors will need to employ more and more strategies from the repertoire that we set out.

Given that students' learning needs do change over time, it is vitally important for mentors to be aware of what stage of development each student is at when they arrive in the school. Students on their first teaching experience will, for example, have very different learning needs from those near the end of their professional preparation and the strategies used by the mentor need to be adapted accordingly. In the first few days of their school placement, the mentor and class teacher will therefore need to ascertain each student's learning requirements for this period of school experience.

Summary

STAGES OF MENTORING

1:   Beginning teaching

- Focus of student learning – rules, rituals and routines; establishing authority
- Role of mentor – model
- Key mentoring strategies – student observation focused on routines and collaborative teaching

2:   Supervised teaching

- Focus of student learning – teaching competences
- Role of mentor – trainer
- Key mentoring strategies – observation by the student; systematic observation and feedback on competences of performance by the mentor

3:   From teaching to learning

- Focus of student learning – understanding pupil learning; developing effective teaching
- Role of mentor – critical friend
- Key mentoring strategies – student observation; re-examining lesson planning

4:   'Reflective' teaching

- Focus of student learning – developing independent reflective practice
- Role of mentor – co-enquirer
- Key mentoring strategies – partnership teaching; partnership supervision

3.1: Beginning teaching

During this stage, students are learning to *see*; that is to disentangle and identify some of the complexities of the teaching process. One of students' initial priorities is to establish effective class control, but in trying to understand how teachers go about this, students face two particular difficulties.

The first is that, by the time students arrive in school (often part way through the year), teachers already have a well-established relationship with their pupils. Much of the work that goes into achieving order takes place at the very beginning of the school year and thereafter is implicitly understood by teacher and pupils alike. Secondly, teachers often have difficulty in explaining how it is that they achieve class control. To experienced teachers, class control is seen as a *natural* process and one that is difficult to discuss in isolation from other aspects of their practice.

Because much of what students most want to learn is so complex and invisible to the untutored eye, we would suggest the focus for students in the earliest stages of learning to teach should be on the rules, routines and rituals of the classroom. By observing, discussing and copying these ready-made strategies, students can more quickly begin to act like teachers and take on an authoritative role in the classroom.

HOW CAN TEACHERS SUPPORT STUDENTS IN THESE EARLY STAGES OF LEARNING TO ACHIEVE CLASS CONTROL?

Some suggestions:

Act as a model for students

By using focused observation and collaborative teaching, class mentors are acting very much as a model for students:

- interpreting events;
- guiding their seeing;
- drawing students' attention to what they are doing and why; and
- to the significance of what is happening in the classroom.

Select topics for student observation and collaborative teaching

For example, ask students to observe:

- the start of the day – what pupils are expected to do when they come into the classroom – how the pupils are settled – how activities are introduced etc;

- how pupils' attention is gained;
- how expectations concerning pupil movement and noise are conveyed;
- what pupils are supposed to do when they have finished their set tasks, rules about collecting and returning resources;
- how the class mentor concludes the teaching session and oversees the pupils leaving the classroom.

Or ask students to identify and record:

- how the class mentor's authority is maintained – e.g. by constant attention to minor infringements of established rules;
- how the class mentor's authority is restored when it is more directly challenged through disobedience or disruption;
- the form of the class mentor's requests in relation to work;
- the form of class mentor's requests in relation to behaviour.

N.B. Experienced teachers are usually direct and precise when giving instructions about work but indirect in their requests in relation to pupils' behaviour – making use of humour, for example. Inexperienced students often do the exact opposite!

Once students have observed these and similar routines, they can become the focus of collaborative teaching episodes. Students can, for example, be asked to take responsibility for:

- managing the distribution of resources;
- beginning and/or ending a teaching session;
- managing the transition from one activity to another.

Collaborative teaching also allows students the opportunity to gain an initial experience of whole class teaching while class mentors remain responsible for class management and control.

3.2: Supervised teaching

Once student teachers have gained some insight into the rules, routines and rituals of the classroom and, through carefully supported collaborative work, have themselves had some experience of teaching the whole class, they will be ready for a more systematic approach to training. During this second phase of their teaching experience, students are likely to be mostly concerned with developing their own performance as teachers; their aim will be to achieve greater and greater control over the teaching and learning process. This development can be supported if mentors explicitly develop a formal training role, focusing directly on the *competences* of teaching.

In reality, teaching cannot be fully characterized as a series of discrete competences – the whole is always more than the sum of the parts. To extract one particular element from a complex process like teaching is necessarily artificial. Nevertheless, for training purposes there are considerable benefits in mentors focusing on specific teaching competences in a systematic and structured way.

HOW CAN MENTORS MAKE BEST USE OF COMPETENCES IN TRAINING STUDENT TEACHERS?

Some suggestions:

Establish a regular programme of observation and feedback

Systematic training based on the competences of teaching should build on the strategies outlined in the last section. Students need to observe and be observed, though this observation should be tightly focused.

Establish a tight focus for training

In terms of the content of training, the broad focus is provided by the government criteria listed under the headings of:

- whole curriculum;
- subject knowledge and application;
- assessment and recording of pupils' progress;
- pupils' learning;
- teaching strategies and techniques; and
- further professional development.

(Full details of these criteria are provided on pages 85–87.)

However, particular courses and individual mentors may well wish to add to the list provided. Moreover, all students will benefit from some experience of more tightly focused support than is implied in the government's list. The competence of *questioning* provides a useful example of how this can be achieved.

According to the government list of competences, newly qualified teachers should be able to *communicate clearly and effectively with pupils through questioning, instructing, explaining and feedback* (2.6.8). Such a written statement in reality involves many *competences* and will need to be broken down before it can be used for training purposes. In promoting the development of questioning technique, you might begin by directing students to undertake focused observation of an experienced teacher on a range of possible dimensions of questioning techniques; this could be followed up by sequenced observation and feedback on students' own questioning technique by class mentors.

The following are examples of specific questions that might be addressed by mentors (or equally by students) in their observations:

- Why is the teaching strategy of questioning being used? (What is the student trying to find out or wanting the children to learn?)
- Is it appropriate for this purpose?
- Who is chosen to answer questions? (Is this appropriate?)
- How long does the student wait for an answer?
- What does the student do if an incorrect or inappropriate answer is given (rephrase, prompt, ignore etc.)?
- How do pupils respond to the questions?
- Does the student appear interested in the pupils' responses/ideas?
- Are questions appropriately pitched?
- Are open and closed questions used appropriately?
- What *intellectual work* do the questions demand (recall, repetition, reformulation, interpretation, etc.)?
- In her/his questioning has the student taken into account the demands of the subject area? (See, for example, activity 9.6.)

Clearly, many of the government criteria can usefully be focused in this way. The degree of specificity of guidance you need to give the student will vary depending on the stage of student development and on past achievement in successfully acquiring competences. The more difficulty a student has, the more helpful it is for you to give specific guidance.

The open observation schedule on page 73 provides a useful framework for such systematic observation.

3.3: From teaching to learning

Once students have gained basic competence and confidence in the classroom, they should begin to *decentre* – that is, to turn their attention away from their own performance and look more deeply at the quality of pupils' learning and appropriate ways of teaching to support that learning.

Developing the ability to *decentre* is a vitally important part of becoming an effective teacher. However, experience shows that unless they are given some direct help, students often fail to move on in this way – their learning tends to reach a plateau. The purpose of this section is to provide some suggestions so that mentors can help students move forward at this time.

Students who have difficulty in moving on to consider the quality of pupil learning often have problems in common.

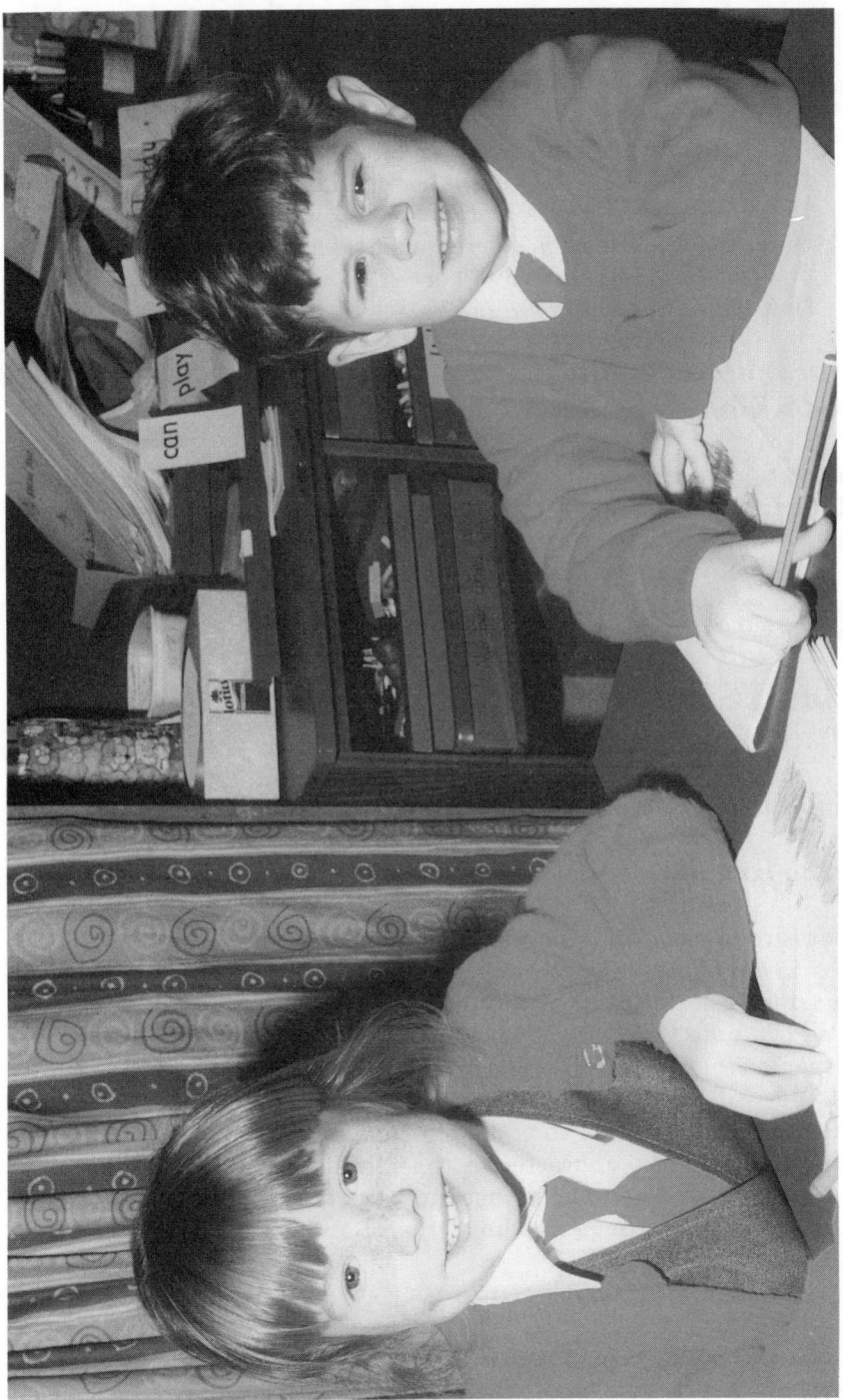

Figure 3.1: From teaching to learning

They may hold views that are not supportive of this switch in focus

For example, they may believe:

- that teaching is simply about the transmission of knowledge and the accumulation of factual information;
- that children are blank slates;
- that school learning is *discrete* and separate from learning going on elsewhere in pupils' lives; or
- that giving correct answers denotes understanding.

They may not have enough confidence in their own classroom management and control

An appreciation of how pupils' learn demands a willingness to experiment with different strategies of classroom organization. In particular, it demands that pupils take an active role in their learning and, when appropriate, participate in investigation and inquiry. For some student teachers, especially those who have only a tentative hold on classroom control, this may appear very threatening.

WHAT STRATEGIES CAN MENTORS USE TO HELP STUDENTS FOCUS MORE DIRECTLY ON PUPIL LEARNING?

Some suggestions:

Adopt the role of a 'critical friend'

If students are to move on to develop a more realistic understanding of the processes involved in effective teaching and learning, they need to be encouraged to look critically at the teaching procedures they have established and evaluate their effectiveness.

However, as they are often still extremely insecure about their teaching abilities, they will need considerable support if they are going to undertake this. The task of mentors is thus doubly challenging at this stage of students' development. We characterize the role as being a *critical friend*. Mentors needs to be able to challenge students to re-examine their teaching, while at the same time providing support and encouragement.

Discuss lesson plans with students

Students can be asked to plan a lesson or sequence of lessons in advance of the weekly mentoring session. At the session, discussion should be focused on the *content* of the planned lesson rather than on the *performance* of the student.

For example, mentors may wish to ask their students:

- What *exactly* do you want the pupils to learn and *why*? (Students frequently focus on what pupils are to *do* rather than on what they are to *learn*);
- What do the pupils know about the specified *learning* already and how do you intend to build on this understanding?
- How are you going to support and structure pupils' learning?
- How appropriate are the teaching strategies you have chosen for supporting this learning?
- How is the activity to be differentiated to meet particular pupils' learning needs? (What are the different ways in which work can be differentiated?)
- What formal assessment opportunities have been identified?

> Who is to be assessed?
> How will you assess?
> What will your role be while you are assessing?
> What will count as evidence of understanding/competence?
> What will you do with the information you gain?

- What attitudes, learning and study skills does this activity encourage?
- Does the activity reflect an understanding of the nature of this subject area and its underlying processes (for example AT1 in mathematics and science)?

Arrange for students to observe pupils working

In their observations students need to focus their attention very specifically on how pupils learn. Mentors might encourage this switch in focus by, for example, asking students to:

- observe pupils when they are engaged in practical activities, taking note of, for example, how particular pupils tackle their work;
- observe pupils of differing abilities and try to understand the learning strategies each is using;
- engage a small group of pupils in discussion in order to explore their understanding of a particular task or concept;
- devise an activity that requires pupils to transfer an earlier piece of learning to a new context.

Undertake the activities outlined in Part B of this booklet

Activity 6.4 requires student teachers (who will probably be at an early stage of their school experience) to make an initial exploration of pupils' thinking and understanding. The majority of activities in Sections 7, 8 and 9 aim specifically to help students understand the complexities of pupil learning in each of the subjects of the core curriculum. The English activity 7.5, for example, asks students to observe a small group of pupils who are engaged in a writing activity and make note of the strategies they use when they are unable to spell a word. Having analysed these pupils' writing and identified common spelling errors, students are asked to devise games and strategies to develop individual children's spelling skills. It is noted in Section 10 of this handbook that one student commented that undertaking this activity helped her to focus on the *pupils*. rather than on *her performance* and on the *process* of pupil learning as well as on the *outcomes* of the lesson.

It is important to recognize that students will only slowly develop a more sophisticated understanding of the processes involved in teaching and learning. It may well be necessary to return to some or all of these questions on a number of different occasions with students.

3.4: 'Reflective' teaching

There is one further stage of student development that needs to be considered: their development as independent reflective practitioners. Many of those in HEIs argue that students' ability to reflect upon their practice should be enhanced throughout a course of training; right from the first day on their course, students should be encouraged to read; to assess; and to think critically; about all aspects of the educational process. We do not disagree. However, we suggest that there is an important difference between learning *about* teaching and learning *to* teach. Much of what goes on in a university or college concerns learning *about teaching* and it is right and proper that the issue is addressed in a manner appropriate to higher education. The HEI-based aspects of professional preparation should involve reflection, analysis and open-minded critique.

Our concern in this handbook is rather different; it is with the practical process of *learning to teach* that takes place in school. Learning how to reflect on and critically evaluate one's own teaching is a vitally important aspect of professional development; if students are not supported in developing these abilities in school, then no amount of university or college-based work will turn them into independent reflective practitioners. But we have found that students are unlikely to be able to address the more fundamental issues underlying their practice until they are able to stand back from their performance and have begun to engage with the complexities of pupil learning. That is to say, students initially may be able to reflect only on *how far they have achieved* the stated purposes of the activities they plan for their pupils. When students have gained basic confidence and competence in their teaching and, with the mentors' support, they may be able to move on to evaluate the *quality and appropriateness* of these purposes. However, it is only at this later stage of their professional development that students may be able critically to evaluate the *significance* of these purposes: to reflect on the underlying social, moral and political issues that are relevant to the activities they plan and teach. This is what we understand by being an *i*ndependent reflective practitioner.

HOW CAN MENTORS PROMOTE THE DEVELOPMENT OF STUDENTS AS INDEPENDENT REFLECTIVE PRACTITIONERS?

Some suggestions:

Develop a more advanced focus for student learning

The definition of reflective practice is highly contentious. Nevertheless, we suggest that the focus for student learning in this final stage of development should include:

- broadening students' repertoire of teaching strategies;
- encouraging students to take more responsibility for their own professional development;
- deepening students' understanding of the complexities involved in teaching and learning, including its social, moral and political dimensions;
- encouraging students to develop an analytical and self-critical approach to practice.

Adopt the role of 'co-enquirer'

As students begins to acquire greater skill and knowledge and to develop a more appropriate and realistic understanding of the nature of teaching, so mentors should begin to modify their role yet again. While there will still be times when mentors act as *model*, *trainer* or *critical friend*, they should also develop the role of *co-enquirer*. As co-enquirers, mentors will have a more open and equal relationship with students, spending more time working as equal professionals. Such a relationship has the advantage of encouraging students to take greater responsibility for their own learning and allows both students and mentors to address some of the complexities of teaching in a spirit of open enquiry.

Use the key mentoring strategies – partnership supervision and partnership teaching

Partnership supervision and *partnership teaching* are in many ways similar to the strategies of systematic observation and feedback and collaborative teaching outlined earlier in Section 2. However, at this point in students' training, these strategies should be developed in ways appropriate to a more equal professional relationship between students and mentors.

Partnership supervision

In partnership supervision it is students, rather than mentors, who select the focus for mentors' observations. The topics students choose can vary widely. They may, for example, wish to sharpen particular classroom skills such as the use of praise or handling group work; they may wish to experiment with a new teaching strategy or piece of work. Whatever the focus, students must be encouraged to take responsibility for selecting it. It is the task of mentors merely to observe students, record evidence (the open observation schedule on page 73 may be helpful here) and provide feedback afterwards.

The strategic use of partnership supervision in the later stages of school experience can do much to encourage students to take responsibility for their own professional development and, careful analysis of the observational evidence provided by mentors, can help students learn how to evaluate their own practice. As a strategy, partnership supervision complements and extends student self-assessment and action planning (see Section 4).

Partnership teaching

Once students have gained considerable confidence in their own teaching, there are advantages in their returning occasionally to teaching alongside their class mentors. As in collaborative teaching, student and mentor should engage in a cycle of joint planning, joint teaching and reviewing, though in each case the roles they adopt are likely to be more equal than in the early stages of professional preparation.

Partnership teaching can have many uses. For example, it might be used to encourage students to broaden their repertoire of teaching strategies, or to allow students to experiment with new teaching techniques. However, its most valuable role is in providing a context for discussion of planning and teaching at a more fundamental level than before. This can be achieved by mentors discussing:

- the complexity of the thinking underlying professional decisions;
- the moral, practical and other dilemmas underlying these decisions;

- the broader consequences of particular decisions;
- the social, institutional and political context in which professional decisions are made.

It is by participating in such open discussions in relation to their own practice that mentors and class teachers can encourage students to confront the complexities of teaching more deeply. If such discussions are linked to an HEI-based programme of reading and writing then the students will indeed become truly reflective practitioners.

Section 4

Student Assessment

Introduction

In the past, even though schools were centrally involved in supporting students in the development of their practical teaching competence they were not always fully involved in assessment procedures. Most tutors did make it a regular practice to consult teachers before reaching any assessment decisions and disagreements between teachers and those in higher education were rare. Nevertheless, although they may have been consulted, teachers were not usually given any formal responsibility for assessment. Government reforms have fundamentally altered this situation, and schools now have the opportunity to work in full and equal partnership with HEIs in the assessment of students.

Like any form of educational assessment, a scheme for assessing student teachers must allow a range of different objectives to be met. It must:

- give guidance on both formative and summative assessment;
- be able to respond to the different stages of student development (as outlined in Section 3);
- encourage and facilitate student self-assessment;
- ensure that students achieve common minimum standards of performance on the key competences.

In this section, we have drawn on procedures developed by Michael Rowe as part of the University of Wales Swansea's PGCE Partnership Scheme. In setting out our suggestions, we are not necessarily advocating that others adopt them in their entirety. Rather we intend that schools, and perhaps those in higher education, will draw on them selectively in the development of their own assessment practices.

WHO SHOULD BE INVOLVED IN THE ASSESSMENT PROCESS?

As part of the partnership scheme, the role and responsibility of the school in the assessment procedure should be negotiated and defined. But even

61

when the school's role is clear, it will still be necessary to decide who in the school is to be involved in the assessment process. We would suggest that all of those working directly with students – the senior mentor, the class mentor and whoever takes on the role of subject mentor – should be involved in regular formative assessment.

However, we would also suggest that in most cases, it is the senior mentor who should take on primary responsibility for more formal, summative assessment; this should be the case even though individual class mentors have taken an active role in mentoring *their* students. Our reason for this suggestion is that experience has shown that taking on the assessment role changes the nature of a class mentor's relationship with a student. It necessarily introduces an element of formality into that relationship and as a result, some class mentors have found it undermines the strong personal support that they wish to give their students. Having an *outsider* who still knows the student very well can therefore be an advantage, though clearly where the senior mentor is also the class mentor, then this is not possible.

Schools need to recognize that whoever takes on the responsibility for formal assessment will be taking part in a process that will at times be personally challenging. This is inevitably so in a small institution like a primary school – particularly when students are weak or are in danger of failing. However, we would hope that if the partner schools work in close collaboration with each other and with the HEI and if they adopt and develop some of the procedures and criteria we have outlined below, then assessment will, in most cases, prove a productive part of the mentoring process.

We begin by giving examples of observation schedules that have been devised for use at different stages of students' development; each of these schedules may be used for assessment both during (formative assessment) and at the end (summative assessment) of the student's teaching experience. We then go on to consider procedures for profiling, student self-assessment and action planning.

4.1:   Observation schedules

An important strategy in the assessment of student teachers – and one that has been used by teachers and tutors for many years – is the observation schedule. If carefully developed and sensitively used, observation schedules can provide a valuable framework for mentors, and can also act as a device for helping students in their own self-assessment and action planning. However, if they are to be effective, then observation schedules need to be developmental too. Included in this section are a series of observation schedules that are intended to be used in a developmental way.

OPEN OBSERVATION SCHEDULE (PAGE 73)

The open observation schedule may be used to provide specific feedback on a particular issue. Initially, when students have limited understanding of teachers' practice, it is appropriate for mentors to select the focus for attention. However, at a later stage in students' development, the same schedule can be used to provide feedback to students on issues they themselves have selected for particular attention. This schedule will also enable senior mentors to monitor whether assessments are being made in a range of different contexts – for example, when students are managing pupils' practical investigations as well as more formal didactic teaching sessions – and in relation to different aspects of students' practical teaching competence.

COMPETENCY-BASED OBSERVATION SCHEDULE (PAGE 74)

This observation schedule is derived from the government's list of competences (DFE Circular 14/93; WO Circular 62/93). A further list of competences devised by the TTA/OFSTED is likely to be published in the near future. Whatever competences are eventually defined as appropriate to newly qualified teachers these will need to be carefully considered by schools and HEIs. The following points might form the basis for such considerations:

- how might individual competences be *interpreted* – what, for example, is understood by *awareness of how pupils learn* and the various factors that affect the learning process?
- which competences are most appropriate for particular assessment purposes – *formative* and *summative* assessments?
- what counts as evidence of competence in each case – what do we mean by *effective* and *appropriate*?
- what level of competence do we expect at particular stages of students' school-based development?

Competences can be an important tool in both formative and summative assessment. We believe they are valuable in that:

- students are made aware of the criteria on which they are to be assessed;
- they provide a means of identifying areas of students' strengths and weaknesses:
- they provide a means of measuring students' progress; and
- they provide a framework for setting targets for future development.

Competency-based observation schedules may be particularly appropriate when students have gained some insight into the rules, routines and rituals of the classroom and are ready for a more systematic approach to training.

PUPIL-FOCUSED OBSERVATION SCHEDULE (PAGE 76)

This schedule draws on the OFSTED/OHMCI school inspection framework and is intended to focus on the quality of pupils' learning and learning outcomes rather than on the student's performance. It is particularly appropriate for use in the later stages of students' school experience when mentors are encouraging students to *move from teaching to learning*. After mentors have undertaken the observation, students should be asked to consider and comment on aspects of their teaching that they consider were of particular significance to the quality of pupils' learning. In this way students will be encouraged to make important links between pupils' learning and their own expectations and practice.

As part of the process of encouraging student teachers to focus more directly on pupils' learning, students may themselves use such a schedule to observe their class mentors or possibly another student teacher.

4.2: Profiling, self-assessment and action planning

Observation schedules, though valuable, are not in themselves a sufficient basis for student assessment in a school-based scheme. Such observation procedures need to be incorporated into a profiling procedure which is itself linked to student self-assessment and action planning.

Profiling is valuable in that it formally and concisely charts students' progress over the whole period of training. In addition, it can provide an important link between students' initial teacher training and their induction and further professional development. We believe that profiling is considerably strengthened if it is undertaken in a way that develops students' abilities to assess themselves and to devise plans for their own further professional development. It is for this reason that periodic profile review meetings should be undertaken by senior mentors and should be combined with self-assessment and action planning. These are similar procedures to those now being introduced in many schools as part of the appraisal process.

How can self-assessment and action planning be linked to profiling?

Some suggestions:

Hold occasional formal reviews of progress

Action planning by students needs to grow out of a careful review of their progress to date. Formal profile review meetings need be held only occasionally; they may, for example, be scheduled to take place at the end of each block teaching experience. If possible, it is beneficial if the HEI tutor can be part of the profile review.

In preparation for the profile review, senior mentors will need to assemble a range of different sorts of *evidence* on students' progress. However, if students are to have ownership of the action plan arising from the review, they too must be involved in assessing their own progress. As a preliminary to the formal review, students should therefore be asked to undertake a self-assessment exercise.

Support students in self-assessment

Self-assessment by students does have its limitations. Students' evaluations of their developing competence will necessarily be *framed* according to:

- their particular (and possibly limited) understanding of teaching and learning;
- the perceived expectations of mentors and tutors;
- their capacity for critical analysis; etc.

In addition, students may find it difficult to acknowledge their strengths and, in particular, their weaknesses.

However, we believe that despite these limitations students should be helped to make formal evaluations of their progress and attainment. Becoming centrally involved in their own assessment, students are likely to feel an increased sense of commitment to developing their professional competence and understanding. In addition, involvement in this process will support students in their development as effective self-assessors – this will be crucial if they are to continue to progress throughout their teaching career.

We suggest that there are three steps to effective self-assessment:

> 1) the senior mentor asks the student to complete a self-assessment schedule (see pages 77–81);

2) the student uses the completed self-assessment schedule as an aid to completing a profile review form (see page 82);
3) the profile review form is used to record particular strengths, areas of significant weakness and also aspects of the student's practice which need further experience.

Students may also benefit by being reassured and seeing teaching and learning in greater complexity – for example, their recognition of the many tensions and dilemmas inherent in teachers' practice – is evidence of progress!

Assemble other appropriate evidence

Appropriate evidence and documentation should be brought to the profile review meeting.

The student should bring:

- the completed self-assessment schedule;
- the completed profile review form;
- her/his school experience file;
- her/his school portfolio (if appropriate).

The senior mentor should bring:

- copies of completed observation schedules;
- notes/written reports from the class mentor and subject mentor;
- copies of any earlier action plans.

Undertake the profile review

If students are to benefit from the review process and use it as a basis for action planning then the following principles need to be observed:

- students and senior mentors both need to be well prepared;
- the meeting needs to be conducted in privacy without interruptions;
- adequate time needs to be given – at least 30–45 minutes;
- senior mentors should try to observe the '80/20 Rule' – encouraging students to talk for at least 80 per cent of the time;
- senior mentors need to develop the skills of:

  listening;
  questioning;
  analyzing;
  summarizing; and providing feedback.

At the end of the profile review, the senior mentor will need to help the student identify challenging but attainable targets for the next phase of her/his development, and to identify how and when these targets might be achieved. The senior mentor should also complete a formal profile review form, a copy of which can be entered in the students' school development records (see Section 2.1).

Figure 4.1: Discussing an action plan

WHAT IS IT IMPORTANT TO CONSIDER WHEN DRAWING UP AN ACTION PLAN?

Content

The content of action plans can be quite variable; they may, for example, include:

- Things a student plans to do in the next phase of her/his school experience. For example:

  > improving specific teaching skills;
  > employing a wider range of teaching methods;
  > focusing on particular curriculum areas;
  > making greater use of IT;
  > becoming more involved in extra-curricular activities.

- Things a student wishes to find out more about. For example:

  > knowledge of subject content;
  > SATs;
  > home–school links;
  > pupil transitions (nursery/infant; infant/junior; junior/secondary).

- *Skills* a student wishes to develop. For example:

  > handwriting;
  > voice projection;
  > displaying children's work;
  > use of audio-visual aids.

It is important that students are encouraged to identify those aspects of practice that are relevant to them at their particular stage of development.

Structure and presentation

If they are to be useful to students in guiding their development, action plans need to be written in an appropriate format. That means that they must include:

- targets that are specific and realistic;
- a programme of action;
- a time scale.

4.3: Dealing with failing students

When we say students are having *difficulties* with their practice we generally mean that their level of knowledge, understanding and skill falls below that which is to be expected of students at a particular stage of their development. Often the effectiveness of students' classroom control is considered inadequate, or the content of the activities they plan for the pupils is considered inappropriate or trivial. Some students' difficulties appear to be related to their *attitude*. For example, they seem not to appreciate the demands of being a professional educator. The most difficult group of students to deal with are those who display certain personality characteristics which, in the judgement of other professionals, may make them unsuitable for entry into the teaching profession. Most common in this category are those students who appear unwilling or unable to establish themselves as a *presence* in the classroom. While many students who have difficulties early on in their practice do eventually reach a satisfactory level of competence, others do not and become *failing* students. In either case, dealing with students who are having severe difficulties can be both challenging and time consuming for all concerned.

WHAT SHOULD BE DONE IN THE CASE OF STUDENTS WHO ARE HAVING DIFFICULTIES?

Some suggestions:

Inform the HEI tutor

The HEI tutor should be made aware from an early stage that there are concerns about a student's practice and informed of the precise nature of these concerns. Discussions on the best course of action should take place between the HEI tutor and the senior mentor. It may be appropriate to involve the class mentor and possibly the student teacher in these discussions.

Try to determine students' particular difficulties

Unless students' particular difficulties are ascertained they cannot be addressed. Sometimes these difficulties are not immediately apparent. For example, students who appear to be having difficult with classroom control may in fact misunderstand the nature of the teachers' role: they may not appreciate that they cannot simply be the pupils' friend. Occasionally, a student's difficulties may be exacerbated or even, in extreme cases, be caused by a personality clash with the class mentor. In such cases the senior mentor will need to discuss with the HEI tutor whether the student would benefit from changing classes or even moving to a different school.

Keep an open mind

As stated above, many students who display difficulties at an early stage of their practice can be helped to make progress and to eventually reach a satisfactory level of competence. There *are* dangers, therefore, in labelling students as failures too early on in their training course; it is important to keep an open mind in the initial stages of students' school experience.

Support students

It is likely (but not always the case) that students are acutely aware that they are having difficulties. This usually has a negative impact on students' confidence and can exacerbate their problems. As with all learners, you need to set appropriate and reasonable goals and praise students' achievements. This may mean giving students extra support in the classroom: more collaborative teaching experiences for example.

Be honest with students

At the same time as supporting students, you will need to be honest about their progress and level of attainment. You should acknowledge and discuss students' difficulties and continue to support their development whilst also making it clear that at some stage an assessment will be made of their practical teaching competence.

Keep detailed records

It is imperative that all records which document students' progress are adequately detailed and that at each stage honest judgements are made about their progress. This is particularly true in the case of a student who is in danger of failing their final school experience.

Ensure that class mentors are given extra support by the senior mentor

While senior mentors will probably take responsibility for formally assessing students, it is class mentors who are likely to be most involved with their students and who will need the greatest on-going support. Class mentors may need:

- help in deciding how to support students' development whilst also protecting the best interests of the pupils;
- advice on how to encourage students whilst not giving them false hope of passing the school experience;

- reassurance that it is not their fault if, despite all their efforts, students fail to reach the required level of competence.

Ensure the school is given extra support from the HEI

Maintaining a professional attitude towards students, and balancing the supportive and assessment roles is extremely challenging in the case of a student with severe difficulties. This should not be the sole responsibility of the school. Extra support should be available from HEI tutors who may, for example:

- work directly with student teachers;
- make additional informal or formal assessments of students' competence;
- support class mentors in their work with students;
- support senior mentors in assessing students' competence, in working with class mentors and in writing students' school experience report.

On some occasions it becomes obvious to all those concerned that a student is not going to reach the level of competence required to pass the block teaching experience. This is likely to be distressing for the student, particularly if this is her/his final teaching experience.

WHAT SHOULD BE DONE IN THE CASE OF A FAILING STUDENT?

Some suggestions:

Keep the student informed

If towards the end of the school experience it is considered that a student is unlikely to *pass*, then s/he should be notified of this fact. This will need to be handled sensitively but at the same time, there is a need to be specific about the reasons for the likely failure. If it is not the student's final teaching experience, then s/he should receive counselling and advice from the senior mentor or HEI tutor. Students who fail their final teaching experience should be informed by the HEI of the likely implications of this failure and of their rights of appeal.

Writing the school experience report

At the end of the block teaching experience the school will most likely be asked to submit a report outlining students' attainment and giving a recommendation of pass or fail in terms of their practical teaching competence. This report may be written by the senior mentor in conjunction with the HEI tutor although in some partnership schemes the senior mentor will have sole responsibility for this task. If the school is recommending that a student should fail her/his teaching experience you will need to make clear:

- the reasons for this recommendation – this should be set out clearly and with adequate detail;
- whether you feel the student should be given the opportunity for a further or extended school experience;
- if (as may happen in extreme cases) the nature of the student's difficulties is such that her/his continuation is considered detrimental to the development of the pupils.

'Open' Observation Schedule

Name:	**Date:**
Year group:	**School experience:**

Context of observation:
(e.g. whole/part of lesson; whole class/group; nature of activity; subject area; support available.)

Main focus of observation:

Notes and comments:

Key issues for attention:

Signed (mentor/tutor)   **Signed (student)**

Aspects commented on (please tick):

Lesson planning & preparation	☐	Pupils' learning	☐
Subject knowledge & application	☐	Class management & control	☐
Teaching strategies & techniques	☐	Assessment and recording	☐

Competency-based Observation Schedule

Name: **Date:**

Year group: **School experience:**

A: Lesson Planning and Preparation

		VG	G	S	U
Lesson plan	– thorough? clear? adequate detail?				
Learning objectives	– appropriate? clear?				
Lesson content	– appropriate? purposeful? continuity and progression?				
Subject knowledge / Knowledge of NC requirements	– confident? accurate?				
Lesson structure	– clear? variety of teaching/learning strategies?				
Resources	– selection, preparation, organization?				

B: Teaching strategies and techniques

		VG	G	S	U
Lesson beginning	– effective? Purpose of lesson clearly conveyed?				
Communication	– intonation? clarity? enthusiasm?				
Teaching strategies a) explaining b) instructing c) questioning d) feedback	– range? appropriateness? relevance? effectiveness?				
Timing and pace	– effective? purposeful?				
Flexibility	– modification of approach if necessary?				
Use of blackboard	– neatness? clarity?				
Use of IT	– competence?				
Lesson conclusion	– purposeful? effective?				

C: Pupils' Learning

		VG	G	S	U
Expectations of pupils	– appropriately demanding?				

(VG = very good; G = good; S = sound; US = unsatisfactory)

Classroom environment	– purposeful? supportive? orderly? attractive?				
Relationship with pupils	– supportive? appropriate?				
Differentiation	– appropriate? responds to individual differences?				
Interest and motivation	– maintained? learning opportunities exploited?				
Development of learning/study skills	– encouraged?				
Development of positive attitudes	– encouraged?				
Management/organization (e.g. group work/ whole class teaching)	– appropriate for learning objectives?				
Attainment of learning objectives	– achieved?				

D: Class management and control

		VG	G	S	U
Expectations of behaviour	– clearly conveyed? appropriate?				
Discipline	– praise/encouragement? – appropriate standards/ use of sanctions?				
Talk/movement	– appropriate? able to gain attention?				
Awareness of pupils	– maintained?				
Sense of authority	– established/maintained? professional distance?				

E: Assessment and recording

		VG	G	S	U
Pupils' understanding	– monitored during lesson?				
Feedback (oral/ written)	– constructive?				
Formal assessment opportunities	– planned? rigorous? refer to NC?				
Pupils' progress	– monitored/recorded				

Additional notes and comments:
(Continue on reverse of sheet)

Signed (mentor/tutor)   **Signed** (student)

Pupil-focused Observation Schedule

Name:	**Date:**
Year group:	**School experience:**

Summary of lesson:
(Including specified learning objectives)

Quality of pupils' learning:
(e.g. pupils' attitudes, interest, understanding of task, concentration, discussion of ideas and information, co-operation, development of learning skills and strategies – e.g. information seeking, posing questions, applying understanding to new situations, evaluating work)

Quality of outcomes/achievement of learning intentions:
(e.g. development of knowledge, understanding and skills, attainment of individual pupils, assessment/record keeping)

Signed (mentor/tutor)   **Signed** (student)

Students should use the reverse of this sheet to comment on aspects of their teaching that were particularly significant to the quality of pupils' learning and outcomes.

Self-assessment Schedule

Use this checklist to evaluate yourself for each item.

A: **Lesson Planning and Preparation**	VG	G	S	US
1: Plan lessons thoroughly and in adequate detail	☐	☐	☐	☐
2: Ensure learning objectives are clear and appropriate	☐	☐	☐	☐
3: Ensure learning objectives take account of continuity and progression of pupil learning	☐	☐	☐	☐
4: Demonstrate confident subject knowledge	☐	☐	☐	☐
5: Demonstrate secure knowledge of NC requirements and school policy documents	☐	☐	☐	☐
6: Ensure lesson content is purposeful and relevant	☐	☐	☐	☐
7: Consider teaching strategies and methods of curriculum/classroom organization in relation to particular learning objectives	☐	☐	☐	☐
8: Structure lessons clearly using a variety of teaching/learning strategies	☐	☐	☐	☐
9: Select, prepare and organize resources carefully	☐	☐	☐	☐

B: Teaching strategies and techniques

	VG	G	S	US
1: Ensure lesson beginnings are effective	☐	☐	☐	☐
2: Ensure that the purpose of lessons are clearly conveyed	☐	☐	☐	☐

	VG	G	S	US
3: Speak clearly, varying the tone, volume and pace of speaking	☐	☐	☐	☐
4: Give clear instructions and explanations	☐	☐	☐	☐
5: Effectively question individuals and the whole class	☐	☐	☐	☐
6: Manage a range of teaching/organizational strategies including whole class teaching	☐	☐	☐	☐
7: Ensure work is paced appropriately	☐	☐	☐	☐
8: Modify approach/teaching strategies if necessary	☐	☐	☐	☐
9: Write neatly/accurately on the blackboard	☐	☐	☐	☐
10: Use IT as part of teaching and learning	☐	☐	☐	☐
11: Communicate enthusiasm	☐	☐	☐	☐
12: Ensure the conclusion of lessons are purposeful and effective	☐	☐	☐	☐

C Pupils' Learning

	VG	G	S	US
1: Ensure expectations of pupils are appropriately demanding	☐	☐	☐	☐
2: Ensure the classroom environment is purposeful and orderly	☐	☐	☐	☐
3: Ensure relationships with pupils are supportive and appropriate	☐	☐	☐	☐
4: Respond to individual differences	☐	☐	☐	☐

	VG	G	S	US
5: Ensure interest and motivation is maintained	☐	☐	☐	☐
6: Exploit all learning opportunities	☐	☐	☐	☐
7: Ensure the development of learning/ study skills	☐	☐	☐	☐
8: Ensure the development of positive attitudes towards learning	☐	☐	☐	☐
9: Achieve stated learning objectives	☐	☐	☐	☐

D Class management and control

	VG	G	S	US
1: Clearly convey expectations of pupil behaviour	☐	☐	☐	☐
2: Appropriately praise and encourage pupils	☐	☐	☐	☐
3: Use appropriate sanctions	☐	☐	☐	☐
4 Ensure talk and movement are purposeful	☐	☐	☐	☐
5: Gain the attention of the whole class when required	☐	☐	☐	☐
6: Maintain an *awareness* of pupils	☐	☐	☐	☐
7: Project a sense of authority	☐	☐	☐	☐

E Assessment and recording

	VG	G	S	US
1: Monitor pupil understanding when teaching	☐	☐	☐	☐

	VG	G	S	US
2: Give constructive oral/written feedback	☐	☐	☐	☐
3: Plan formal assessment opportunities and ensure these are rigorous and refer to NC	☐	☐	☐	☐
4: Make use information gained in lesson planning	☐	☐	☐	☐
5: Effectively monitor and record pupils' progress	☐	☐	☐	☐

F Wider Professional Role

	VG	G	S	US
1: Establish good working relationships with colleagues and with parents	☐	☐	☐	☐
2: Respond appropriately to advice offered and show a willingness to develop professional knowledge, understanding and skills	☐	☐	☐	☐
3: Show a willingness to assume responsibility and take initiative	☐	☐	☐	☐
4: Ensure you are punctual and reliable	☐	☐	☐	☐
5: Manage time effectively	☐	☐	☐	☐
6: Evaluate teaching effectiveness	☐	☐	☐	☐
7: Contribute to extra-curricular activities	☐	☐	☐	☐
8: Identify and provide for a diversity of talent, for pupils with special educational needs and those with specific learning difficulties	☐	☐	☐	☐

	VG	G	S	US
9: Show a readiness to promote the spiritual, moral, social and cultural development of pupils	☐	☐	☐	☐
10: Show vision, imagination and creativity in educating pupils	☐	☐	☐	☐

Signed   **Date**

(VG = very good; G = good; S = sound; US = unsatisfactory)

Profile Review Form

Name:	**Date:**
Year group:	**School experience:**

A: Lesson planning and preparation

e.g. clarity of learning objectives, subject knowledge, knowledge of NC requirements/schemes of work; preparation and organization of resources.

B: Teaching strategies and techniques

e.g. starting and ending lessons, maintaining pupils' interest and motivation, teaching strategies and techniques, methods of organization, use of IT.

C: Pupils' Learning

e.g. expectations, relationships, understanding of how pupils' learn, achievement of stated learning objectives.

D: Class Management and Control
e.g. sense of authority, awareness of pupils; use of praise and encouragement; ability to gain pupils' attention.

E: Assessment and Recording
e.g. informal/formal assessment, oral/written feedback, monitoring pupils' understanding, recording of pupil progress.

F: Wider Professional Role
e.g. relationship with colleagues and parents, time management, contribution to extra-curricular activities, evaluation of teaching effectiveness.

G: General comments

Signed   **Date**

Action Plan Form

Name		Date	
Year group		School experience	

Target	Programme of action	Target date

Signed (mentor)   **Signed** (student)

Signed (tutor)

continue on reverse of sheet if necessary

Government Criteria for Initial Teacher Training (primary phase)
(DFE Circular 14/93: Welsh Office Circular 62/93)

2: COMPETENCES EXPECTED OF NEWLY QUALIFIED TEACHERS

2.1: Higher education institutions, schools and students should focus on the competences of teaching throughout the whole period of initial training. The progressive development of these competences should be monitored regularly during training. Their attainment at a level appropriate to newly qualified teachers should be the objective of every student taking a course of initial training.

CURRICULUM CONTENT, PLANNING AND ASSESSMENT

a: *Whole Curriculum*

2.2: Newly qualified teachers should be able to:

2.2.1: demonstrate understanding of the purposes, scope, structure and balance of the primary curriculum as a whole;

2.2.2: ensure continuity and progression within the work of their own class and with the classes to and from which their pupils transfer;

2.2.3: exploit, in all their teaching, opportunities to develop pupils' language, reading, numeracy, information handling and other skills.

b: *Subject Knowledge and Application*

2.3: Newly qualified teachers should be able to:

2.3.1: demonstrate knowledge and understanding of the subjects of the primary curriculum which they have studied, at a level which will support effective teaching of these subjects;

2.3.2: use that knowledge and understanding to plan lessons, teach and assess pupils in the core subjects of the National Curriculum and those other subjects of the primary curriculum covered in their course; newly qualified teachers may need some guidance and support in some of these subjects.

c: *Assessment and Recording of Pupils' Progress*

2.4:   Newly qualified teachers should be able to:

2.4.1:   test, assess and record systematically the progress of individual pupils;

2.4.2:   judge how well each pupil performs against appropriate criteria and standards by identifying individual pupils' attainment, with reference to relevant National Curriculum requirements;

2.4.3:   use such testing and assessment in their planning and teaching;

2.4.4:   provide oral and written feedback to pupils on the processes and outcomes of their learning;

2.4.5:   prepare and present reports on pupils' progress to parents.

TEACHING STRATEGIES

a: *Pupils' Learning*

2.5:   Newly qualified teachers should be able to:

2.5.1:   identify and respond appropriately to relevant individual differences between pupils;

2.5.2:   show awareness of how pupils learn and of the various factors which affect the process;

2.5.3:   set appropriate and demanding expectations of their pupils;

2.5.4:   devise a variety and range of learning goals and tasks and monitor and assess them.

b: *Teaching Strategies and Techniques*

2.6:   Newly qualified teachers should be able to:

2.6.1:   establish clear expectations of pupil behaviour in the classroom and secure appropriate standards of discipline;

2.6.2:   create and maintain a purposeful, orderly and supportive environment for their pupils' learning;

2.6.3:   maintain pupils' interest and motivation;

2.6.4:   present learning tasks and curriculum content in a clear and stimulating manner;

2.6.5:   teach whole classes, groups and individuals, and determine the most appropriate learning goals and classroom contexts for using these and other teaching strategies;

2.6.6:   use a range of teaching techniques and judge when and how to deploy them;

2.6.7: employ varying forms of curriculum organization, and monitor their effectiveness;

2.6.8: communicate clearly and effectively with pupils through questioning, instructing, explaining and feedback;

2.6.9: manage effectively and economically their own and their pupils' time;

2.6.10: make constructive use of information technology and other resources for learning;

2.6.11: train pupils in the individual and collaborative study skills necessary for effective learning.

FURTHER PROFESSIONAL DEVELOPMENT

2.7: Newly qualified teachers should have acquired in initial training the necessary foundation to develop:

2.7.1: a working knowledge of their contractual, legal, administrative and pastoral responsibilities as teachers;

2.7.2: effective working relationships with professional colleagues (including support staff) and parents;

2.7.3: the ability to recognize diversity of talent including that of gifted pupils;

2.7.4: the ability to identify and provide for special educational needs and specific learning difficulties;

2.7.5: the ability to evaluate pupils' learning, and recognize the effects on that learning of teachers' expectations and actions;

2.7.6: a readiness to promote the spiritual, moral, social and cultural development of pupils;

2.7.7: their professional knowledge, understanding and skill through further training and development;

2.7.8: vision, imagination and critical awareness in educating their pupils.

Part B

Subject Mentoring in the Primary School: the Core Curriculum

Edited by Trisha Maynard, Sue Sanders and John Furlong

Section 5

Ten questions about subject mentoring

Introduction

If subject mentoring is to be purposeful and effective, then there are a number of key issues that need to be considered and addressed. The aim of this section is to draw attention to these issues and also to provide some guidance for schools and higher education institutions (HEIs).

5.1: WHAT IS SUBJECT MENTORING?

In the introduction to this handbook, we clarified the particular terminology we are using and our understanding of the terms *class mentor* and *senior mentor*. We also noted that the role of the *subject mentor* is rather different. The role of the subject mentor is to focus specifically on the development of student teachers' knowledge, understanding and skills in the teaching of one or several of the National Curriculum subject areas.

This role may be fairly easy to define but it is much more challenging to implement within the primary school! This is because subject mentoring is not likely to be undertaken by just one person who becomes the designated *subject mentor*, but by several colleagues. These colleagues will be required to work collaboratively, discussing their practice and sharing their particular expertise. Who might take on this role and how subject mentoring might be organized in the primary school are addressed in Question 7, below.

5.2: HOW HAS SUBJECT MENTORING IN THE PRIMARY SCHOOL COME ABOUT?

Two factors may be of particular significance to the introduction of subject mentoring.

- We noted earlier that school experience is now recognized as a fundamental part of their professional preparation. In addition, the unique contribution that teachers acting as mentors can make to students' development is also acknowledged and valued. Partnerships between schools and HEIs are consequently an essential feature of ITT.

- It is widely recognized that the National Curriculum has provided primary school teachers with many challenges in the way of subject understanding. This appears to be the case particularly for teachers of Key Stage 2 (KS2) pupils.

Given these two factors, it is unsurprising that Circular 14/93 (WO Circular 62/93) stipulates that from September 1996, students are required to spend a minimum of 150 hours of *directed time* on the teaching of each of the core areas of the National Curriculum and that *directed time* may be spent either in schools or in HEIs. Indeed, as we noted earlier, this Circular specifically recommends that schools should play a greater role in student teachers' curriculum and subject studies.

If schools are to become involved more formally in developing students' knowledge and skills in the teaching of the core curriculum, it is important initially to examine the kinds of knowledge that teachers need in order to teach subjects effectively.

5.3: WHAT KINDS OF KNOWLEDGE DO TEACHERS NEED IN ORDER TO TEACH SUBJECTS EFFECTIVELY?

It is generally agreed that teachers need to have a good personal knowledge of subject areas – that is, they need to have a sound understanding of the facts, concepts, procedures, skills etc., that they are required to teach their pupils. They also need to have a sound understanding of a subject's key ideas and its underlying processes. These processes generally relate to the kind of understandings found in the National Curriculum Attainment Target 1 (AT1) for mathematics and science. In addition, teachers' practice may be influenced by the particular understandings they hold about the nature of the subject they are teaching. This is another aspect of personal subject knowledge it is important for teachers to consider if they are to be effective in their work with pupils.

But having a personal knowledge of the subject area, however thorough, is not enough. In order to teach effectively, teachers need to find ways of making the subject content accessible to their pupils. This kind of knowledge – *subject knowledge for teaching* or *subject application* – draws on teachers' personal subject understandings but also on their knowledge of pupils and of pupil learning. Subject knowledge for teaching incorporates understandings about, for example, the processes involved in learning to read or pupils' early understanding of number. It also incorporates understandings about, for example:

- tried and tested *good* ideas for pupil activities;
- pupils' common difficulties with learning a particular aspect of subject content and ways of dealing with these difficulties;
- curriculum resources; and
- how to manage and organize the teaching of a practical activity or investigation.

It is apparent, therefore, that the knowledge teachers hold that enables them to teach subjects effectively is diverse and draws on a range of different kinds of understandings. When we use the terms *subject knowledge* and *subject mentoring* therefore, we are not referring specifically or solely to teachers' personal subject knowledge. Rather, we are referring to the broader range of subject understandings needed for teaching to be effective.

5.4: WHAT ARE STUDENT TEACHERS' COMMON DIFFICULTIES WITH SUBJECT KNOWLEDGE?

Student teachers may lack a sound personal knowledge of the subjects they are required to teach and also of how pupils develop understanding in particular subject areas. They may, for example, only have a tentative grasp of the key ideas and underlying processes of mathematics, or what is known about pupils' early development of numeracy. Indeed, student teachers often appear, at least initially, to consider these issues to be irrelevant to the activities they plan and teach on school experience.

In addition, student teachers' beliefs about the nature of teaching and learning may have a profound effect on how they view the subject content of their activities. These beliefs are likely to be based on students' own memories as pupils – significant teachers and lessons, how they believe they were taught and how they believe they learn best. Many students initially regard teaching simply as *telling* and learning as *remembering*. Other students may see the role of teacher as more of a *facilitator* of pupil learning – but in either case it is likely that they will view teaching and learning as something that *just happens* without a great deal of effort on their part.

These beliefs and lack of subject knowledge can have profound consequences for students' planning and practice – their *subject application*. For example:

- Students may not appreciate the differences between their own and their pupils' thinking about the subject content and may therefore attempt to impose their personal and abstract ways of understanding on the children. For example, a diagram of the water cycle may make perfect sense to the student teacher but as an introduction to an understanding of water in the environment it is unlikely to mean a great deal to younger primary pupils. Students may also fail to consider the importance of exploring pupils' ideas about concepts before planning and teaching activities (see, for example, Section 10 – Science – Activity 1).

- Students may isolate and decontextualize learning. Rather than devising a situation where the learning has a real purpose and makes sense to the pupils, students often isolate the learning from any context, breaking it down into little steps and teaching these one at a time. This particularly appears to be the case with some writing activities, where the importance of *purpose* and *audience* are neglected.

- Students often collect *good ideas* for activities – from curriculum guides; from their teachers and tutors; and even from their own memories of being a pupil. However, they often use these *good ideas* inappropriately: they fail to determine the specific concept being addressed; or how the activity they are teaching relates to their understanding of what the subject area is about. For example, students may claim that making bread is a *nice thing to do* with KS1 pupils, seeing the activity as *i*nteresting and fun rather than a way of furthering children's understanding of particular mathematical and scientific concepts.

- Students may be so focused on ensuring pupils reach the *right answer* that they teach them *shortcuts* or *empty procedural tricks* – for example:

  if you're multiplying by ten an easy way is to add a nought.

  Student teachers may also fail to consider the process of pupil learning – for example, the strategies pupils use in attempting to reach a solution – and the implications this has for teachers' planning (see, for example, Section 10 – English – Activity 5).

- Students may fail to consider the ways of working associated with the subject area when planning their activities – what it means to work like a writer or a scientist, for example. Even when these underlying processes are considered, they may be seen not as indicative of the way the activity should be structured and taught, but as something separate from the subject content – you teach the knowledge one day, the processes and skills another. Alternatively, while students may be aware of these processes they may feel reticent about integrating them into their teaching plans (see, for example, Section 10 – Mathematics – Activity 4).

It is only in the face of experience and constant, constructive challenge and guidance that many students move on to develop more complex and appropriate understandings about their practice. This is what makes subject mentoring in the primary school so important!

5.5: WHAT CONTRIBUTION CAN TEACHERS MAKE TO STUDENTS' SCHOOL-BASED SUBJECT STUDIES?

It is important to emphasise that the activities in Part B of this handbook are intended to enhance, contextualize and develop students' college-based subject studies and not to replace them. There is bound to be some overlap between students' college-based and school-based studies. For example, some aspects of the teaching of the core curriculum areas – subject application – will probably be addressed in both schools and in HEIs, though from different perspectives. Similarly, while the development of students' personal subject understandings may not be the specific aim of school-based work, through a consideration of how they are going to make subject content accessible to their pupils, students are likely to develop their personal subject knowledge. Student teachers often comment that in order to teach something you have really to understand it yourself first! The overlap therefore, between student teachers' college-based and school-based studies should only serve to enrich students' professional development.

However, teachers are also in a position to develop student teachers' subject knowledge in a way that other interested professionals can not. Teachers hold detailed and sophisticated understandings about the children they teach, the contexts in which they are working and of how best to develop their pupils' subject understandings. Drawing on this knowledge, teachers are able to make an invaluable and unique contribution to students' professional preparation.

5.6: WHAT ARE THE DEMANDS OF SUBJECT MENTORING?

Essentially, there are two main demands of subject mentoring – these relate to *subject knowledge* and *time*.

Subject Knowledge:

It is possible that some teachers may express concern about focusing on *subject knowledge*. These colleagues may need to be reassured that becoming involved in mentoring subject knowledge does not necessarily signal a move towards single subject teaching, or the end of the generalist class teacher. Nor is it about training students to focus on factual knowledge and didactic teaching methods. Rather, it is about developing and strengthening students' subject understandings so as to enable them to become more effective primary teachers.

Other teachers may be reticent to become involved in this work as they are concerned about their personal subject expertize. These teachers may be anxious that they will be required to develop student teachers' understandings of particular aspects of subject content about which they feel rather vulnerable. Obviously, much will depend on how subject mentoring is organized within the school (see Question 7). However, colleagues can be reassured that the subject specific activities in Section 7–9 of this book are concerned with general conceptions of good practice within the teaching of each of the core curriculum areas. The activities in these sections do not, for example, prescribe particular mathematical or scientific concepts that should form the basis of mentors' work. Rather, they are intended to be adapted and *used* with whatever aspect of subject content the subject mentor considers appropriate.

Time

This is an important issue and we have already noted that if mentoring is to be effective then there needs to be adequate time allocated for working with students. In devising these materials we have tried, as far as is possible, to minimize this demand – for example, by ensuring that activities generally require little input from the teacher as the student actually undertakes the task. This is not to underestimate the time demands of this work. If subject mentoring is to be meaningful and effective, time is needed for:

- discussing activities with students: an *initial input*, so that students understand the purpose of activities, and a *feedback* session, so that mentors can guide students' thinking and help them to make sense of their experiences;
- working with colleagues;
- liaising with the HEI tutor – negotiating which activities it is appropriate for students to undertake and also for discussing students' progress and attainment.

How *time* demands are managed will depend on various factors:

- the number of students on placement in the school;
- how subject mentoring is organized;
- the amount of funding offered by the partner HEI for undertaking subject mentoring; and
- how this funding is used or allocated within the school.

This is something that certainly needs to be discussed by all those participating in this work. (This issue is discussed in Section 1.6.)

5.7: HOW MIGHT SUBJECT MENTORING BE ORGANIZED WITHIN THE PRIMARY SCHOOL?

An important factor which influences the time demands of subject mentoring is how this work is organized within schools. The issue of organization is particularly pertinent to the activities described in Sections 7–9. These activities are designed to support schools in developing students teachers' understandings in relation to the teaching of each of the core curriculum areas. But:

- Who is best placed to take on the role of subject mentor?
- How is this work most effectively organized within schools?

Unfortunately there are no easy answers to these questions.

However, in most schools it is likely that either class mentors or curriculum co-ordinators will take on this role. Obviously there are advantages and disadvantages in each case. Some of the most important of these are set out below.

Class mentors as subject mentor

Advantages

- There is much greater flexibility of organization – in planning, undertaking tasks and in giving feedback;
- As class mentors work closely with their students and are familiar with the context in which they are working, they may be able to make the tasks and the feedback session much more purposeful, relevant and meaningful to students;
- This method of organization may appear less threatening to many teachers, as they have greater autonomy over their work with students. Some teachers may prefer not to *share* their students or their class with colleagues;
- There may be some opportunities for the professional development of individual class mentors as they focus on subject understandings in the core areas.

Disadvantages

- Class mentors may not have the same level of subject knowledge in all core curriculum areas. In addition, they may not have the same depth of subject expertize as curriculum co-ordinators;
- As class mentors work closely with their students, they may find it difficult to insist that students carry out their tasks – particularly when students claim they have other priorities!

Curriculum co-ordinators as subject mentor

Advantages

- Student teachers may benefit from working with a number of experienced teachers who have particular expertize in the teaching of a core curriculum area;
- Where they do not have students placed in their classes, it may be easier for curriculum co-ordinators to maintain a professional distance from students and so find it easier to be more directive;
- Curriculum co-ordinators could work with groups of students. Not only will students be able to learn from more formally discussing and evaluating each other's experiences but this approach is also more cost effective in terms of time demands – several students can discuss their planning etc. at the same time;
- There may be greater opportunities for professional development within the school as teachers begin to share their subject expertize and discuss their practice.

Disadvantages

- The organization of this work is much more problematic and time consuming;
- Class mentors may feel uncertain about curriculum co-ordinators working directly with their students. Differences in values or ways of working may cause conflict between curriculum co-ordinators and class mentors and tension for the student teacher;
- Curriculum co-ordinators may lack detailed knowledge of students' classes and of the teaching of the curriculum area at a particular Key Stage;
- Curriculum co-ordinators are appointed for a variety of reasons – not always to do with their subject expertize. In addition, in small schools teachers may be asked to act as co-ordinator for several subject areas. In these cases, curriculum co-ordinators may not feel confident and competent in mentoring subject knowledge;
- For the HEI tutor, liaising with all participating curriculum co-ordinators and class mentors may be very time consuming.

Of course, it may be that a combination of these two models is considered most appropriate. That is, on some occasions curriculum co-ordinators work directly with student teachers. This may be with individual students, or with all of the students on placement in the school. On other occasions curriculum co-ordinators take on a more advisory role – supporting class mentors in their work with students. This more flexible way of working, while organizationally challenging, would seem to provide greater opportunities for the professional development of teachers.

While these are the most likely ways of organizing subject mentoring in primary schools, they by no means represent all possibilities. In some contexts, for example, it may be the senior mentor who is considered most appropriate to take on the role of subject mentor. It can only be concluded that this is an extremely complex issue! The important point here is that how this work is organized within each primary school needs careful consideration, preferably by the whole staff. This may form a useful part of a school's programme of preparation for subject mentoring (see Question 9). An example of the possibilities and challenges of organizing subject mentoring is illustrated in Section 10 – Mathematics – Activity 1.

5.8: WHY SHOULD SCHOOLS BECOME INVOLVED IN SUBJECT MENTORING?

Given that subject mentoring does make further demands on teachers, it is quite legitimate for schools to ask why they should agree to become involved in this work – in short, *What's in it for us?*. Teachers who piloted these activities recognized the challenges of this work, but maintained that there are important reasons why schools should become involved in subject mentoring.

Firstly, as with all forms of mentoring, it was felt that through participating in this work schools were able to exert a greater influence on shaping the next generation of teachers. Secondly, teachers acknowledged that involvement in subject mentoring can enhance the professional development of schools and teachers.

But what are the *particular* benefits of subject mentoring?

- In terms of whole-school development, involvement in subject mentoring can highlight those areas in need of improvement – for example, school policies or systems for planning and assessment that are in need of updating and extending.
- Individual teachers can also benefit from involvement in this work. Through using the activities described in Sections 6–9, reflecting on their own understandings in order to work effectively with students, and liaising with curriculum co-ordinators and other subject specialists, teachers should develop their subject knowledge. In addition, through analyzing students' difficulties in a more structured and systematic way, teachers should gain greater insight into their own beliefs and practice. Evaluating *these* should provide teachers with the opportunity to become more effective primary practitioners.

5.9: WHAT CAN BE DONE IN THE WAY OF WHOLE SCHOOL PREPARATION FOR SUBJECT MENTORING?

You should initially refer to Section 1.2 *Preparing the school for partnership* and Section 2.1 *Planning and preparation*. In addition, there are several issues that can be addressed in order to prepare the school specifically for subject mentoring:

- If there is not yet a designated senior mentor in the school, an appropriate colleague should be asked to take on responsibility for the co-ordination of this work. Advice is given on the appointment of a senior mentor in Section 1.4. Depending on how subject mentoring is organized within the school, this person may take on an advisory and supportive role with colleagues or s/he may become more actively involved in mentoring subject knowledge to students;
- The senior mentor should arrange a series of meetings to enable colleagues to discuss issues related to the implementation of subject-based mentoring – for example, colleagues' attitudes towards the role of subject knowledge in the primary school and the advantages and disadvantages of the various organizational models in relation to their particular context. How the time demands of subject mentoring are addressed will also need to be considered;
- The senior mentor should invite a representative from the partner HEI to discuss subject mentoring with all members of staff. Schools will need to ascertain, for example, the expectations of the HEI in terms of the number and range of activities undertaken on students' school experience and what funding and support it is able to offer;
- The senior mentor should find out colleagues' needs in terms of subject knowledge. For example, would colleagues welcome an INSET session on key ideas related to particular core curriculum areas and the development of children's understanding within those areas?
- If the senior mentor has undertaken mentor training s/he could run a session for colleagues, on working with student teachers and mentoring skills and strategies. Alternatively, the partner HEI should be able to provide INSET. In addition, the materials in Section 10 are devised specifically to enable schools to begin to explore the possibilities and challenges of subject mentoring. These materials should be read in conjunction with the relevant activities described in Sections 7–9 of this handbook.

5.10: HOW CAN THE ACTIVITIES DESCRIBED IN SECTIONS 6–9 BE MOST EFFECTIVELY USED TO SUPPORT SUBJECT MENTORING?

The activities described in Sections 6–9 should not be seen as a series of exercises to be worked through slavishly from beginning to end. Rather, they are intended as a resource to support schools and HEIs in developing student teachers' subject knowledge while on *school experience*. Which activities are used, when they are used, how they are used and whether tasks are repeated at a later stage, will depend on students' learning needs and the particular contexts in which they are working. These decisions will need to be negotiated between individual schools and HEIs.

As a general guide, however, activities in Section 6 are likely to be particularly appropriate when students are in the early weeks of their school experience – possibly when they are on initial *observation* days or as part of a serial practice. These activities are intended to provide an early introduction to the complexities of teaching and to some of the principles underlying good primary practice. In relation to the stages of mentoring described in Section 3 of this handbook, they would be most relevant to Stages 1 and 2: *Beginning teaching* and *Supervised teaching*.

Activities in Section 6 are not subject-specific and may be used to promote students' initial understandings within any core curriculum area or indeed, within several areas. It should be noted, however, that it may be inappropriate and unproductive for students to undertake all activities within all core curriculum areas. Rather, mentors may prefer to develop students' understandings of, for example, the demands of effective long-term and medium-term planning in the primary school through a detailed exploration within any one curriculum area.

The activities in Sections 7, 8 and 9 are, on the whole, more challenging and complex. They may therefore be most appropriate for use a little later in students' development and as part of their block teaching experience. In terms of the stages of mentoring described earlier, these activities would be relevant to Stage 2 *Supervised teaching* and, in particular, to Stages 3 and 4: *From teaching to learning* and *Reflective teaching*.

Most of the activities in sections 7–9 focus on key ideas and broad processes and skills associated with these curriculum areas. They can therefore be used with whatever topic, theme, or aspect of subject content the mentor considers to be appropriate. Some of the activities in this section are especially suitable for pre-teaching *observation* days, for example, activity 9.1 asks students to investigate children's understanding of a science concept. This activity should provide students with invaluable information on which to base their future planning. Other activities are *ongoing* and are intended to extend and develop student teachers' understandings over a period of several weeks (for example, English – Activity 7.5).

The most *challenging* tasks for students may be those which are concerned with managing practical *open-ended* tasks (see, for example, Mathematics – Activity 8.4). These activities may be particularly appropriate for use with student teachers on their penultimate or final teaching experience, although much will depend on the strategies mentors use when working with students. Even the most challenging of activities may be *manageable* if the mentor initially models the task for the student and then carefully supports her/his practice in the classroom – through collaborative teaching, for example. This is why it is so important that mentors are aware of the range of mentoring strategies that are available to them and, how these strategies might be used to respond to students' particular learning needs (see Section 2 – *The Process of Mentoring*).

It is highly unlikely that students will undertake all eight activities in each core curriculum area. This is not important – activities within each curriculum area focus on different kinds of understandings and are not in any order of priority. Which activities are used, when they are used and how they are used should ideally be negotiated between schools and HEIs. What is of fundamental importance is that all those involved in subject-based mentoring recognize that activities should be used flexibly and that they should form an integral part of student teachers' school experience. These activities are not intended to be a *straitjacket* but a useful resource that will enable schools and HEIs effectively to structure and support student teachers' school-based subject studies.

Finally, it is important to note that there is nothing unusual or unfamiliar about the activities described in this handbook. Rather, these activities simply highlight and structure much of the good practice already being carried out informally by mentors on students' school experience.

Section 6

An introduction to good primary practice

Activity 6.1: Long-term and medium-term planning

PURPOSE OF ACTIVITY:

To develop an initial understanding of the need for long-term and medium-term planning, how these plans are developed within schools and how they subsequently influence and support teachers' weekly or daily (short-term) planning.

Task Guidelines

INITIAL INPUT:

The mentor should:

- ensure that the student has access to a copy of the school's long-term and medium-term planning documents for a core curriculum area;
- facilitate a meeting with the appropriate curriculum co-ordinator(s).

TASK:

The student should:

- familiarize her/himself with the content of the relevant school documentation and compare this with the National Curriculum requirements for the relevant subject area.

FEEDBACK:

The mentor should discuss:

- how s/he uses the long-term and medium-term planning documents to support her/his weekly and daily (short-term) planning.

Guidelines for curriculum co-ordinator

The curriculum co-ordinator should discuss:

- how National Curriculum requirements have been interpreted in the appropriate planning documents;
- other issues that influence long-term and medium-term plans, e.g. issues specific to individual schools, statutory assessment at the end of each key stage etc.;
- how these plans provide a structure that facilitates coverage, progression, balance, coherence and continuity within, across and between key stages.

NB It is assumed that, in terms of the particular subject area for which they are responsible, curriculum co-ordinators will have taken a key role in devising the school's long-term and medium-term plans and in managing and organizing shared school resources. This activity, and activity 6.5, therefore, incorporate contributions from both the mentor (who may be the class mentor or senior mentor) and the curriculum co-ordinator.

Activity 6.2: Short-term planning

PURPOSE OF ACTIVITY:

To develop an initial understanding of the importance and demands of short-term planning.

Task Guidelines

INITIAL INPUT:

The mentor should:

- ensure the student has access to the detailed, short-term plans for the previous or current week.

TASK:

For each of the core curriculum areas the student should identify and make note of:

- the different activities taught throughout the week;
- the learning objectives of these activities.

FEEDBACK:

Focusing on notes the student has made on the above points, the mentor should:

- discuss the amount of time allocated within the week to teaching the core curriculum;
- identify whether activities within each core curriculum area are part of long-term on-going work; concerned with the learning of a discrete *topic*; and/or linked to work in other curriculum areas;
- discuss why detailed daily and/or weekly plans and records are necessary to ensure effective day-to-day teaching and assessment.

Activity 6.3: Planning individual activities

PURPOSE OF ACTIVITY:

To develop an initial understanding of the demands of planning effective learning activities.

Task Guidelines

INITIAL INPUT:

The mentor should:

- arrange for the student to observe a group (or groups) of pupils engaged in a practical activity;.
- provide the student with an outline plan of the activity.

TASK:

The students should:

- identify the learning objective that forms the basis of this activity;
- consider how the initial *concept* to be learned has been *interpreted* – i.e. how the class teacher has ensured that the learning is relevant and meaningful to pupils;
- consider how the activity reflects key ideas and underlying processes (ways of working) associated with the curriculum area.

FEEDBACK:

The mentor should discuss:

- the importance of having clear learning objectives for activities;
- how the specified learning was interpreted and embedded in a context which is relevant and meaningful to pupils – i.e. the need to take into consideration pupils' experiences, understanding, ways of thinking etc.;
- how key ideas associated with the subject area and pupils' development of understanding within this subject area were taken into consideration;
- how the activity met individual pupils' learning needs;
- why student teachers should plan pupil activities in detail.

Activity 6.4: Exploring pupils' thinking and understanding

PURPOSE OF ACTIVITY:

To explore pupils' thinking and their understanding of a specific concept or procedure.

Task Guidelines

INITIAL INPUT:

The mentor should:

- arrange for the student to observe a small group of pupils involved in a practical, collaborative activity.

TASK:

The student should:

- observe and make note of pupils' comments and questions as they carry out the activity;
- when pupils have finished the activity, ask them questions about its purpose, what they were trying to find out, what they have learned etc.;
- consider how s/he would use the information in planning further work for pupils.

FEEDBACK:

The mentor should discuss:

- the importance of giving pupils a clear purpose for their work;
- the ways in which individual pupils approached the activity;
- the contribution of discussion to pupil learning;
- how *experience* does not necessarily equate with *understanding*;
- the importance of differentiating the learning objectives of activities according to pupils' needs;
- appropriate ways of furthering pupils' understanding of the specified learning and dealing with pupils' difficulties.

Related activities

(Mathematics activity 8.3 and science activity 9.1)

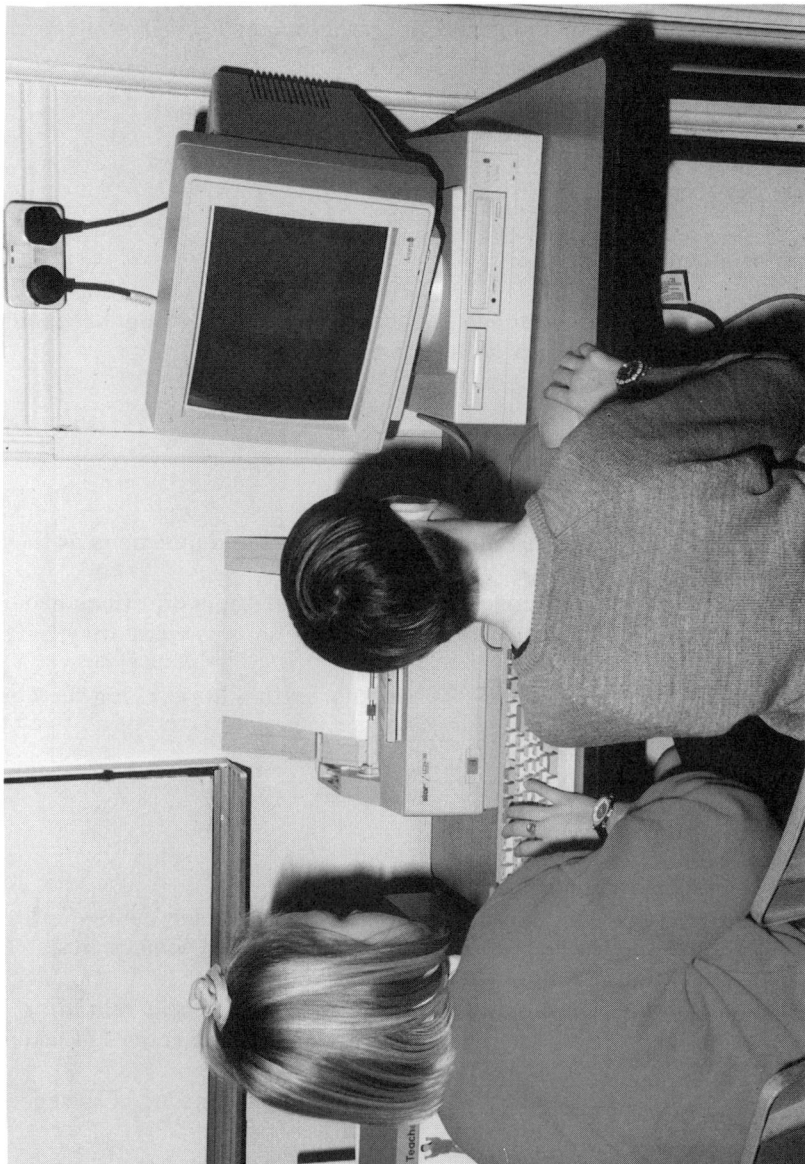

Figure 6.1: Pupils involved in a practical, collaborative activity.

Activity 6.5: Exploring resources within the school and classroom

PURPOSE OF ACTIVITY:

To learn about the management of resources within the school and classroom.

Task Guidelines

INITIAL INPUT:

The mentor should:

- arrange for the student to examine the management and location of resources within the classroom (including IT);
- provide the student with general information about the management and location of shared school resources;
- facilitate a meeting with the appropriate curriculum co-ordinator(s).

TASK:

The student should:

- note where shared school resources are stored and how they are managed;
- note where resources for different curriculum areas are located in the classroom and how they are used by pupils.

FEEDBACK:

Discussion should aim to help the student understand:

- that planning must take account of resource requirements;
- the reasons for the particular arrangement of resources in the classroom;
- the class rules for use of resources.

Guidelines for Curriculum Co-ordinator

Discussion should focus on:

- how shared and subject-specific resources are managed within the school – quantity, accessibility, location;
- the storage and use of particular subject-specific resources.

Related activity

Mathematics activity 8.6

Activity 6.6: Exploring good primary practice

PURPOSE OF ACTIVITY:

To begin to explore some key aspects of effective and appropriate primary practice through involvement in collaborative teaching.

Task Guidelines

INITIAL INPUT:

The mentor should:

- from the short-term plans, identify an aspect of content within one curriculum area;
- plan a whole class activity with the student, or explain to the student the purpose and development of an activity already planned.

TASK:

Depending on the stage of development, the student should either:

- observe the class mentor and help with, for example, the distribution of resources; or
- take a more active role in teaching – taking responsibility for teaching one particular aspect of the lesson.

FEEDBACK:

The mentor should discuss the reasons why this activity might be considered appropriate and effective. For example:

- the reason why whole class teaching is appropriate for this activity;
- the importance of detailed planning and assessment;
- the careful preparation and use of resources (including IT);
- the need for the specified learning to be embedded in a context that is meaningful and relevant to these pupils;
- the need to consider the appropriateness and effectiveness of the activity both in terms of pupil learning and the demands of subject areas;
- the different teaching strategies used during this activity (for example, explaining, questioning, demonstrating);
- how the specified learning might be developed in the future.

111

Section 7

Activities for subject mentoring – English

Activity 7.1: Individual reading

PURPOSE OF ACTIVITY:

To develop the student's understanding of the reading process and the various approaches that s/he can use to help children become effective readers.

Task Guidelines

INITIAL INPUT:

The mentor should:

- select a small group of children with whom this activity can be sustained over several weeks;
- model for the student the process of listening to a child read.

TASK:

The student should:

- ask a child to select a familiar book to share with her/him. At KS1 this may be a simple picture book or a book that the teacher has read to the class. At KS2 this may still be a picture book but could equally well be a chapter from a novel.

FEEDBACK:

The mentor should discuss:

- whether the student was able to support the child's independent reading appropriately, e.g. encouraging the use of a range of cueing systems to decode the text rather than immediately telling the child the word;
- whether the student was able to sustain a discussion focused on the text and if not, how this might have been developed.

The following may provide a useful framework for the student:

- Talk about the book jacket, title and author and discuss what the book might be about;
- Ask the child to read ('read') to you. At KS1 the child may be re-telling the story in her/his own words, reading from memory or reading with support (shared/paired reading). Independent readers could be helped to use cueing systems (semantic, syntax, phonic). At KS2 the child will be reading more independently but may still need support outlined as above (at appropriate points stop to discuss the plot, characters, vocabulary, setting, format etc.);
- Ask the child to reflect orally about likes/dislikes, author, style, plot etc.;
- Ask the child to record her/his reflections. At KS1 this may be pictorial with the teacher as scribe whereas at KS2 the observations may be in the form of a review or recommendation. These reflections can form part of a diary to be maintained by the child during the student's teaching experience. Parental comments in the diary about the child's reading are to be encouraged;
- Record simply what each child knows/understands about reading. Make notes about the kind of teaching/ experiences that might be necessary for the child to make progress.

Relevance of activity for pupils/student teacher

- This strategy of interactive reading has been shown by research to be an effective way of developing reading skills and positive attitudes towards reading. It is wholly consistent with the requirements of the National Curriculum and endorsed by HMI in recent reports on reading (e.g. DES 1992)

Useful References

Barrs, M and Thomas, A. (1991) *The Reading Book*, London: Centre for Language in Primary Education.

Moon, C. and Raban, B. (1992) *A Question of Reading* (3rd Edition) London: David Fulton

Moon, C. and Bourne, J. (1994) *Learning to Teach Reading*, (Course E880) Milton Keynes: Open University Press

Figure 7.1: Student listening to an individual child read

Activity 7.2: Story telling/reading

PURPOSE OF ACTIVITY:

To develop the student's story reading skills. This activity also provides a useful introduction to whole class teaching which enables the student to practise class control and discipline in an enjoyable context.

Task Guidelines

INITIAL INPUT:

The mentor should:

- model the process of story telling/reading for the student;
- help the student to identify an appropriate text to tell/read to the children.

TASK:

The student should:

- read the text through carefully;
- rehearse telling/reading the story out loud – considering issues such as clarity, expression, intonation and volume;
- consider how the story will be introduced and also the learning opportunities afforded by the story – for example, vocabulary, print conventions, story structure, style, genre, rhyme etc. (What will you draw attention to and how? When will you ask questions? What will be the nature of these questions?);
- consider whether the story telling/reading could be enhanced by the use of visual aids, such as puppets or artifacts. Large picture books may be particularly useful and effective at KS1;
- if appropriate, consider whether the children might be asked to contribute sound effects, join in repetitive phrases etc.; and finally
- read/tell the story to the whole class.

FEEDBACK:

The mentor should:

- discuss how effectively the text was introduced. For example, did the student discuss the title, author, cover etc.? Did the student ask the children to make predictions about the content? If the student was reading part of a serialized novel, did s/he recapitulate the story so far or encourage the children to make further predictions etc.?

- discuss the student's strengths in story telling/reading and how s/he could improve these skills;
- discuss whether the student made best use of the learning opportunities provided by the story. (e.g. Did s/he stop at appropriate places to encourage prediction and/or attention to print? Did s/he make effective use of open ended questioning to stimulate and sustain lively discussion about the story?)

Relevance of activity for pupils/student teacher

- Effective story telling/reading can be a springboard for many English activities, as well as other work across the curriculum. Listening to well told stories can develop an enthusiasm for literature and poetry as well as developing personal reading skills;
- Asking open ended questions and encouraging purposeful discussion will enhance the reading experience and help children to develop an understanding beyond the literal;
- Discussions linked to stories provide a range of opportunities for developing many of the speaking and listening skills outlined in the National Curriculum programmes of study.

Useful References

Howe, A. and Johnson, J. (1992) *Common Bonds: Storytelling in the Classroom*, London: Hodder and Stoughton

Marriott, S. (1991) *Picture Books in the Primary Classroom*, London: Paul Chapman

Activity 7.3: Non-fiction writing

PURPOSE OF ACTIVITY:

To encourage the student to plan and implement a variety of writing activities linked to different curriculum areas and provide opportunities for a number of different forms of writing, e.g. narratives, notes, messages etc.

Task Guidelines

INITIAL INPUT:

The mentor should:

- ask the student to produce outline plans for writing activities that they might use on their school experience;
- discuss the appropriateness and relevance of these activities, helping students to modify or expand their plans where necessary.

TASK:

The student should:

- devise a variety of writing activities linked to different curriculum areas and which provide the opportunity for different forms of writing;
- discuss and, if necessary, amend their initial plans;
- implement and evaluate the activities.

FEEDBACK:

The mentor should:

- evaluate the appropriateness and effectiveness of the student's activities and whether they support the development of particular forms of writing;
- discuss the importance of providing a meaningful context for writing activities and the significance of identifying the purpose and audience for pupils;
- consider whether, during the course of the teaching experience, the student is providing the opportunity for pupils to undertake a variety of forms of writing across different curriculum areas.

The following are examples of tasks linked to different curriculum areas that provide opportunities for a number of different forms of writing:

- A visit or visitor might lead to activities such as writing a letter (invitation or request); descriptions (introducing context-specific vocabulary); post cards; posters or brochures; diaries; evaluations;
- At KS1, an activity such as making cakes might incorporate making lists of ingredients or instructions (pictorial or written); process writing; evaluation; opinion 'I like the cake with the pink icing'); and invitations (to a tea party);
- At KS2 a Design and Technology task could incorporate lists (of materials); letters (to experts or suppliers); notes on the planning and generating of the design; instructions for making the design; posters; advertisements; invitation to a product launch; design evaluation;
- KS1 children should be encouraged to consider vocabulary and the organization of their writing; KS2 children should be encouraged to consider what style, tone, presentation, layout etc. is appropriate to the intended audience and particular form of writing adopted.

Relevance of activity for pupils/student teacher

> Literacy is not just a performance skill with the written system of language, but a cognitive tool that transforms our capacity for self reflection, mental re-organization and evaluation.
>
> (Whitehead 1990)

Useful References

Curriculum Council for Wales, (1992) *Write to Learn*, Cardiff: CCW.

National Writing Project, (1989) *Writing and Learning*, Walton-on-Thames: Thomas Nelson

Activity 7.4: Speaking and listening

PURPOSE OF ACTIVITY:

To raise the student's awareness of the importance of talk as a means of learning and of careful planning to include a wide variety of purposes and contexts for children's talking and listening.

Task Guidelines

INITIAL INPUT:

The mentor should arrange for the student (during the course of her/his teaching experience) to spend one morning and one afternoon session observing a group of pupils.

TASK:

The student should:

- revisit the National Curriculum requirements for Speaking and Listening for the key stage s/he is teaching;
- during one morning and one afternoon session observe and keep a record of the opportunities presented to develop effective speaking and listening. In each case make note of the curriculum area, the task being undertaken by pupils and also the social context in which they are working (pairs, small groups, teacher led etc.).

The student should consider:

- the ways in which speaking and listening appear to relate to the development of pupils' knowledge and understanding;
- how pupils' speaking and listening differs in relation to the different activities, the purposes of tasks and the social context in which they are working;
- which activities and contexts appear most beneficial in developing pupils' speaking and listening;
- any difficulties pupils experience in listening, in expressing their ideas clearly and effectively and in responding appropriately to others.

FEEDBACK:

The mentor should:

- discuss the significance of talk as a means of learning (for example, of generating, exploring, clarifying, developing, expressing and evaluating ideas) within different curriculum areas;
- discuss the necessity of ensuring children are presented with a wide variety of contexts and purposes for their speaking and listening(for example, describing, explaining, persuading, giving opinions);
- discuss the possible reasons for particular pupil's difficulties in speaking and listening and strategies that might be used to overcome those difficulties and promote effective speaking and listening.

Relevance of activity for pupils/student teacher

- Talk is fundamental to human interaction. By becoming competent and confident communicators children learn to appreciate and value the skills of negotiation and persuasion over those of brute force;
- Talk and learning are intimately connected. The process of articulating a problem can often lead to clarification and talk can be crucial in converting knowledge into understanding;
- Literacy is dependent on a sound foundation of speaking and listening skills.

Useful References

Baddely, G. (Ed) (1992) *Learning Together Through Talk, Key Stages 1 and 2*, (Video Pack) London: Hodder and Stoughton.

Howe, A. (1992) *Making Talk Work*, London: Hodder and Stoughton

Norman K. (Ed) (1992) *Thinking Voices: the work of the National Oracy Project*, London: Hodder and Stoughton

Activity 7.5: Spelling

PURPOSE OF ACTIVITY:

To allow the student to identify the stage that children have reached in their spelling development and to consider and implement effective strategies in order to promote accurate spelling.

Task Guidelines

INITIAL INPUT:

The mentor should:

- identify a group of about six children with whom the student can work throughout their teaching experience;
- ensure that the student is able to spend an initial teaching session observing these children, i.e. that the student is not directly responsible for teaching these children during this session.

TASK:

The student should:

- observe the children in this group and make note of the strategies these children use when they are unable to spell a word;
- collect a sample of writing from these children and analyze the kinds of mistakes they make with their spelling. Try to identify common errors – e.g. letter strings with which they have difficulty, simple word patterns they appear not to recognize etc.;
- consult the National Curriculum requirements for teaching spelling at the appropriate key stage;
- use this information to devise games and teaching strategies to develop individual children's spelling skills.

Students placed in nursery and/or reception classes should collect samples of independent mark making and early attempts at writing from a small group of children. Their teaching efforts should be directed towards devising strategies to encourage these children in the earliest stages of literacy and this may involve much more oral work, such as listening for rhyme, predicting rhymes and making up rhymes, as well as attention to print when reading to and scribing for children.

FEEDBACK:

The mentor should discuss:

- whether the student was able to identify common spelling errors (or evaluate children's independent mark making and early attempts at writing);
- how far the student used this information diagnostically in developing appropriate games and teaching strategies.

Relevance of activity for pupils/student teacher

- Children must have a good grasp of the spelling patterns of English in order to become fluent readers.

Useful References

Mudd, N. (1994) *Effective Spelling: a practical guide for teachers*, London: Hodder and Stoughton.

Activity 7.6: Response to a text

PURPOSE OF ACTIVITY:

To give the student the experience of devising and implementing a comprehension exercise that uses a series of open-ended questions as the starting point for group discussion and analysis of text.

Task guidelines

INITIAL INPUT:

In the early stages of the student's school experience the mentor should model this task for the student, drawing particular attention to the importance of:

- choosing an appropriate text;
- devising appropriate questions and using effective questioning techniques;
- pacing;
- the significance and nature of teacher intervention.

At a later stage in the student's school experience the mentor should:

- provide guidance and support for the student's own attempt at devising and implementing a comprehension activity.

TASK:

The student should:

- devise and implement a comprehension activity that aims to help children develop understandings beyond the literal and begin to understand the writer's use of language. The activity should start with a series of open-ended questions aimed at developing group analysis and discussion of the text.

FEEDBACK:

The mentor should:

- discuss the suitability of the chosen text;
- discuss the appropriateness and effectiveness of the student's questions and questioning;

- discuss the extent to which the student developed the children's understanding of plot, characters, ideas and the like, and also of structure, vocabulary, grammar etc.;
- discuss the student's ability to manage group discussion.

In the first instance it may be appropriate to arrange for the student to work with one group at a time, helping children to take turns, encouraging contributions from all and supporting children's efforts to formulate a common oral response that will be fed back to the whole class:

- At KS1 strategies such as hot seating, role play or drama may be particularly useful. Towards the end of KS1 children may be ready to read and respond in writing. Strategies might include text marking, the use of dictionaries and thesaurus, changing endings, or responding to open-ended questions;
- At KS2 texts could be drawn from a wide range of sources including traditional and modern poetry, newspaper articles, short stories, contentious issues or historical material;
- Questions – which may be oral in the first instance – should encourage the children to consider in detail the quality and depth of the text through discussion of some of the following: plot, characters, style, vocabulary, use of language, author's intentions, bias, rhythm and rhyme.

Relevance of activity for pupils/student teacher

- Effective comprehension activities should encourage children to use their knowledge gained from reading. It should, for example, develop children's understanding of the structure, vocabulary and grammar of the English language. It should also encourage children to respond imaginatively to the plot, characters, ideas, vocabulary, style and organization of language in literature;
- With experience children should move from shared oral analysis of the text to more independent, written analysis of the text.

Useful References

Lunzer, E. and Gardner, K. (1979) *The Effective Use of Reading*, London: Heinemann

Wray, D. (1994) *Literacy and Awareness*, London: Hodder and Stoughton.

Activity 7.7: Higher order reading skills

PURPOSE OF ACTIVITY:

To ensure that the student understands that the teaching of reading extends beyond KS1 and that certain reading strategies have to be planned for and taught explicitly.

Task Guidelines

INITIAL INPUT:

The mentor should:

- emphasize the importance of developing higher order reading skills across the curriculum;
- support the student in planning activities that demand higher order reading skills;
- suggest techniques and strategies that the student might use to teach these skills.

TASK:

The student should:

- devise an activity that requires children to research information related to the class theme or to a topic being studied within a particular subject area. The activity should demand that children use appropriate higher order reading strategies – e.g. skimming, scanning and more focused reading.

FEEDBACK:

The mentor should discuss:

- whether the techniques and strategies chosen by the student were appropriate and effective in developing higher order reading skills;
- how the skills might be transferred to other curriculum areas.

At KS1 this may involve familiarizing children with the differing formats of non-fiction books and introducing them to associated language and skills – for example, alphabetical order, classification systems (e.g. colour coding), contents pages, indexing, glossaries, dictionaries.

In the early stages children may be asked to produce a labelled drawing based on information they have found out on a particular topic and later could make their own simple information booklet on a subject of interest.

At KS2 as well as use of dictionaries, thesaurus, glossaries, contents/index pages, pupils should be taught the following process:

- to identify the precise information they wish to know;
- make succinct notes;
- use the information in a different way – for example to create graphs, lists, diagrams etc.;
- to provide supporting evidence for a discussion or a discursive piece of writing or to produce an information text for a younger age group.

Relevance of activity for pupils/ student teacher

- The development of higher order reading skills are necessary to tackle more challenging and demanding texts and lays the foundation for independent research and learning;
- The student should appreciate that higher order reading skills are skills for life long learning and have very important cross-curricular implications.

Useful References

Curriculum Council for Wales (1994) *INSET activities for developing higher order reading skills at KS2,* Cardiff: CCW

Reid, D. and Bentley, B. (1994) *Reading Non-fiction: Key Stage 2,* Leamington Spa: Scholastic Publications

Southgate, V., Arnold, H. and Johnson, S. (1981) *Extending Beginning Reading*, London: Heinemann.

Figure 7.2: Older pupils are able to practice more focussed reading

Activity 7.8: Story writing (narrative)

PURPOSE OF ACTIVITY:

To make the student aware that all story writing is dependent upon a knowledge of other stories and that children need to be exposed to a wide range of styles and formats in order to provide a rich source of ideas upon which to draw.

Task Guidelines

INITIAL INPUT:

The mentor should:

- aim, initially, to develop the student's understanding of two forms of narrative writing: *stylistic modelling* and *imaginative writing*;
- describe the children's previous experiences in narrative writing and show the student any formats commonly used for planning in the class;
- suggest suitable texts for stylistic modelling. (The mentor may need to model this activity, drawing attention to the choice of text – this is crucial if this technique is to be successful.)

TASK:

The student should:

- devise a small number of activities that focus on stylistic modelling and imaginative writing as ways of promoting narrative writing.

FEEDBACK:

The mentor should discuss:

- the suitability of the chosen text and its adaptation for stylistic modelling;
- the impact and suitability of the stimulus for imaginative writing;
- the success of the student in supporting children in planning, drafting, revising and editing their work.

STYLISTIC MODELLING:

This is a simple means and possible *way in* to effective narrative writing. Its constraints and clear framework enable children to write easily in a range of distinctive styles. After choosing a suitable text for modelling, the student reads the text aloud, drawing attention, for example, to repetitive phrases, particular grammatical constructions, use of simile or metaphor etc. The student may suggest ways in which the text may be reproduced by altering the characters, setting, and subsequent outcomes, whilst maintaining the format and style of the original.

- At KS1 the children might be involved in rewriting part of a story or a simple rhyme or poem. For example, *Dear Zoo* (R. Campbell) – changing the animals and excuses; *Mr Gumpy's Outing* (J Burningham) changing the animals and the actions;
- At KS2 children might be involved in rewriting a rhyme, short story, newspaper account, slogans, advertisements, headlines. Another possibility is researching and rewriting a picture book for a younger audience. For example, the children might research a popular series of books, such as *Meg and Mog* (H Nicoll and J Pienkowski) by drawing up a list of criteria met by all the books in the series (print conventions, colour of pages, inclusion of a spell etc.) and producing their own versions.

IMAGINATIVE WRITING:

The children will need a prompt or a stimulus, which could be a picture, a newspaper headline, an opening sentence, a piece of music, a visit, a poem etc. Children at all stages need to be taught how to plan, draft, revise and edit their work.

- At KS1 children might be taught how to sequence or plan a story using pictures, with the teacher acting as scribe;
- At KS2 the children will need to be more specific in their planning, taking account of the title, setting, characters, beginning, middle and end. The processes of drafting, revising and editing are made easier by the use of computers, which should be used as a matter of course and not merely to improve presentation of finished work.

Relevance of activity for pupils/student teacher

- Children should be able to write in a variety of narrative styles (e.g. realistic, fable, myth, adventure and rhyme). Children

should be encouraged to adopt the role of writer with confidence
and show an awareness of the reader;

- Narrative is one of the most fundamental and powerful ways of
constructing meaning and enriching and making sense of experiences. According to Wells (1986) the reality each one of us inhab-
its is to a very great extent *a distillation of the stories we have
shared*.

Useful References

Hall, N. (1989) *Writing with Reason: the emergence of authorship in
young children*, London: Hodder and Stoughton.

Section References

Burningham, J. (1978) *Mr Gumpy's Outing*, Harmondsworth: Picture
Puffins (Penguin Books).

Campbell, R. (1987) *Dear Zoo*, London: Campbell Blackie

DES (1992) *The Teaching and Learning of Reading in Primary Schools: A
Report by HMI*, London: DES.

Nicoll, H. and Pienkowski, J. (1972) *Meg and Mog* London: Heinemann.

Wells, G. (1986) *The Meaning Makers*, London: Hodder and Stoughton.

Whitehead, M. (1990) *Language and Literacy in the Early Years:
an approach for education students*, London: Paul Chapman.

General Reading

Curriculum Council for Wales (1991) *Literature-centred Approaches at Key
Stages 1 and 2* (TSPE 2) Cardiff: CCW

Curriculum Council for Wales (1992) *Focusing on Folk Tales (Literature-
centred approaches at Key Stages 1 and 2)* (TSPE 9) Cardiff: CCW.

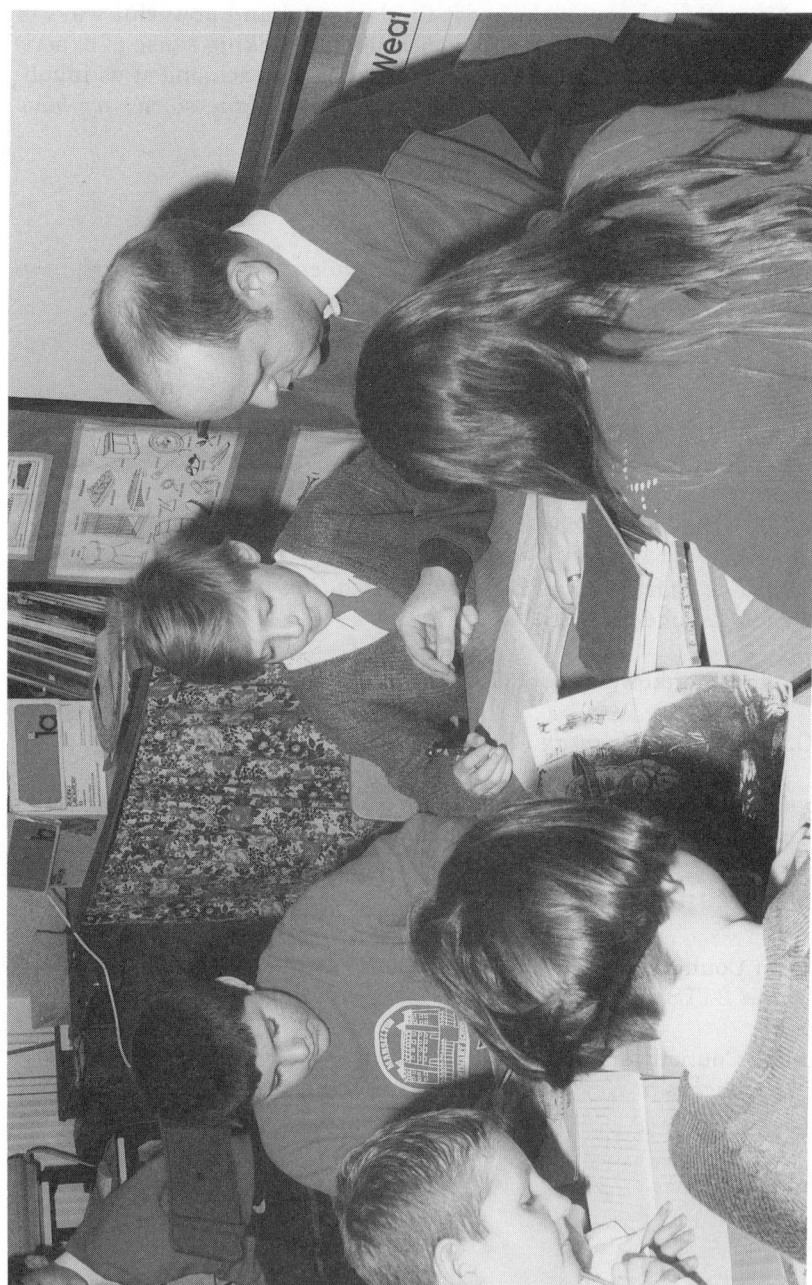

Figure 7.3: Pupil and his teacher discussing an imaginative writing project

Section 8

Activities for subject mentoring – mathematics

Activity 8.1: Using a mathematical game

PURPOSE OF ACTIVITY:

To involve the student in planning and implementing a mathematical game and develop her/his understanding of the purpose and significance of this approach to teaching mathematics.

Task Guidelines

INITIAL INPUT:

The mentor should:

- help the student to identify an appropriate mathematical game;
- suggest whether the game should be played with a group or the whole class and why;
- discuss the attainment and ability of relevant pupils;
- suggest ways of introducing the game;
- suggest ways of recording critical incidents about pupils' mathematical thinking and understanding highlighted during the playing of the game.

TASK:

The student should:

- learn how to play the game;
- implement the game;
- make note of any critical incidents leading to particular insights concerning pupils' mathematical thinking and understanding.

FEEDBACK:

The mentor should:

- discuss the student's evaluation of the planning and implementation of the game;
- discuss the efficacy (ease, accuracy and usefulness) of the recordings and the diagnostic assessments the student has made;
- discuss how this information might influence further teaching plans;
- suggest variations of the game and alternative games.

Relevance of activity for pupils/student teacher

- This activity will help the student to gain insight into the way pupils think about mathematics and develop a repertoire of activities independent of published schemes and workbooks;
- Mathematical games encourage pupils to articulate their mathematical thinking, develop social skills, and consolidate and practice mathematical skills.

Useful References

There are now a wealth of mathematics schemes on the market which give ideas for mathematical games appropriate for use at KS1 and KS2.

In addition, publications such as *Child Education* and *Junior Education* (Scholastic) regularly include suggestions for mathematical games.

Activity 8.2: A mathematical trail

PURPOSE OF ACTIVITY:

To raise the student's awareness of mathematics in the environment and to develop an appreciation of the opportunities and benefits of using real life examples for mathematical learning.

Task Guidelines

INITIAL INPUT:

The mentor should:

- help the student to identify an aspect of work currently being undertaken in mathematics;
- provide information about the mathematical knowledge and attainment of a group of pupils;
- collaboratively plan a trail or evaluate and help the student to modify a trail they have planned before it is tried with pupils;
- provide the student with the opportunity to try the trail with one group of pupils at a time;
- monitor the management of pupils out of the classroom.

TASK:

The student teacher should:

- find out about or revise her/his knowledge of mathematical trails (see suggested references);
- use private study time to explore the school environment for mathematical opportunities;
- devise and implement a well presented and mathematically accurate trail.

FEEDBACK:

The mentor should:

Discuss and evaluate the content, style and presentation of the trail.

For example:

- Did the student carry out adequate preparation?

- Did the trail encourage children to use their mathematical knowledge and understanding to solve real problems?
- Did the trail encourage pupils to work collaboratively?
- Were tasks appropriately differentiated?
- Did the trail stimulate further investigations ?
- What opportunities were provided for assessment ?

Relevance of activity for pupils/student teacher

- Mathematics is concerned with the real world as well as abstract calculations. Pupils should therefore be provided with opportunities to *do mathematics* away from the scheme, workbook and exercise book.
- This activity enables pupils to use and apply their mathematical knowledge – providing different contexts for practice and consolidation.
- Through providing opportunities for creative and collaborative mathematical activity and the communication of mathematical ideas this activity also emphasises the social aspects of the subject.

MATHEMATICAL TRAILS

Mathematical trails are a useful and enjoyable way of contextualizing, using and applying mathematics.

They can be a way of introducing, developing and consolidating all aspects of mathematics. A mathematics trail is similar to a nature or city trail but the focus is on mathematics rather than, for example, on science or local history.

Questions can be teacher or pupil written. Here are a selection from a trail around Swansea Marina.

Questions can be:

a) **Closed**: How many portholes are there on the sailing ship?
b) **Open ended**: What different shapes can you find on the sailing ship?
c) **Investigational**: In how many different arrangements could canon flaps be found opened or shut on the sailing ship?
d) **Problem solving**: How high is the mast on the sailing ship?

Many curriculum guides and teachers magazines include ideas for mathematics trails around school grounds, town and country environments as well as places like historical monuments.

Useful References

Sawyer, A. (1993) *Developments in Primary Mathematics Teaching*, London: David Fulton. See Chapter 2 *Starting Points for Using and Applying Mathematics: Maths Trails*

Selinger, M. and Baker, L. (1991) *The What, Why, How and When of Mathematics Trails*, Derby: Association of Teachers of Mathematics (01332 346599)

Figure 8.1: Using a mathematical game

Activity 8.3: Focusing on an individual learner of mathematics

PURPOSE OF ACTIVITY:

To give the student sufficient time to examine and develop one pupil's understanding and construction of mathematical knowledge.

Task Guidelines

INITIAL INPUT:

The mentor should:

- identify a pupil who is having difficulty with an aspect of mathematics;
- arrange for the student to work closely with that pupil at regular intervals over several weeks;
- support the student in devising an individualized programme of work for the pupil – suggesting strategies and activities that may be appropriate.

TASK:

The student should:

- in relation to one piece of mathematics, assess the pupil's attainment, evaluate her/his understanding and attempt to analyze her/his difficulties;
- devise and implement an individualized programme for the pupil in consultation with the class mentor;
- monitor the pupil's progress and revise the programme as appropriate.

FEEDBACK:

The mentor should discuss:

- the nature of the pupil's difficulties;
- the appropriateness and effectiveness of the programme devised by the student;
- how this programme might be modified in the light of the pupil's progress;

- what the student has learnt about pupils' development of mathematical understanding from this specific case.

Relevance of activity for pupils/student teacher

- Working closely with one pupil should allow the student to gain insight both into how an individual constructs mathematical knowledge and to common misconceptions about mathematics and mathematical learning.

Useful References

Hughes, M. (1986) *Children and Number: Difficulties in Learning Mathematics*, Oxford: Basil Blackwell.

Activity 8.4: Check the rumour

PURPOSE OF ACTIVITY:

To encourage the student, with guidance and support, to devise and implement an open-ended mathematical activity.

Task Guidelines

INITIAL INPUT:

The mentor should:

- suggest or negotiate an appropriate rumour that will lead pupils to undertaking a mathematical investigation;
- suggest appropriate timing, grouping, resources, ways of recording etc.;

TASK:

The student should:

- discuss with the mentor an appropriate rumour that will form the basis of a mathematical investigation;
- plan and implement an activity in which children are told, discuss, test out and then evaluate the rumour (students should consider whether they are able to make use of IT).

FEEDBACK:

The mentor should discuss:

- the challenges of devising and implementing a mathematical investigation;
- the student's interventions – were the student's questions appropriate? Did the student extend pupils' mathematical vocabulary? Did the student ask the pupils to explain and justify their conclusions?
- the student's assessment of pupils' understanding and the implications of this for future mathematics work.

Depending on the aspect of mathematics currently being studied and the age and ability of the pupils the rumour might be:

- It doesn't matter whose feet you use to measure the hall;
- Shapes with the same perimeter all have the same area;
- All numbers in the four times table are also in the two times table but none are in the eight times table.

Relevance of activity for pupils/student teacher

- Conjecture and proof are underlying principles in mathematics. The ability to communicate mathematical ideas is often an under-developed aspect of being a mathematician for pupils;
- Activities of this kind provide pupils with real reasons for discussion about mathematical ideas and provide all pupils (regardless of age, attainment or ability) with the opportunity to make conjectures and explore notions of proof.

N.B. – Undertaking a practical, open-ended task may appear threatening to student teachers – particularly in the early stages of their teaching experience and they may require considerable support and encouragement from the mentor (see Section 10 – Mathematics activity 8.4 – Check the Rumour).

Useful References

Sanders, S.E. (1990) *Early Challengers*, Harlow: Longman.

Activity 8.5: Using mathematical apparatus

PURPOSE OF ACTIVITY:

To enable the student to explore the range of mathematical apparatus/resources kept within the classroom and plan an activity that incorporates the use of one piece of apparatus.

Task guidelines

INITIAL INPUT:

The mentor should:

- identify a skill, concept or investigation that incorporates the use of a piece of mathematical apparatus;
- identify a group of pupils with whom the student should work;
- collaboratively plan an activity or support the student in their planning of an activity.

TASK:

The student should:

- explore the range of mathematical apparatus in the classroom (this may include computer software – for example, *logo* that drives the *turtle*;
- plan and implement an activity that incorporates the use of one piece of mathematical apparatus;
- evaluate the effectiveness of the apparatus with regard to intended learning outcomes for pupils;
- write a short report on the above.

FEEDBACK:

The mentor should:

- discuss the student's report, focusing particularly on the organizational demands of using apparatus and the student's understanding of the use of apparatus in the learning and application of mathematics.

The student may be asked to teach pupils specifically how to use a piece of apparatus e.g. a ruler or a stopwatch. Alternatively, the apparatus may form an integral part of a mathematics activity e.g. investigating place value using Dienes apparatus or investigating number patterns using Multilink.

Relevance of activity for pupils/student teacher

- Apparatus such as Dienes multibase, Multilink and Unifix are widely used in schools to support the learning of basic concepts;
- The skillful use of apparatus such as rulers, protractors and stopwatches as well as calculators and computers can enhance the learning, use and application of mathematics.

Figure 8.2: Playing mathematical games

143

Activity 8.6: Resource audit

PURPOSE OF ACTIVITY:

To enable the student to familiarize her/himself with the range of resources available to support the teaching of mathematics.

Task Guidelines

INITIAL INPUT:

The mentor should:

- negotiate access to shared school resources;
- negotiate and support the sharing of the student's report within the school.

TASK:

The student should:

- explore and prepare a brief report on the range of resources available to support the teaching of mathematics (including IT);
- disseminate the report within the school – this may be to other students or to teachers.

FEEDBACK:

The mentor should discuss:

- the use of shared resources within the school;
- the appropriateness and effectiveness of particular resources in relation to the teaching and learning of specific mathematical ideas, concepts and skills.

EXTENSION ACTIVITY:

The student should:

- choose one resource and within a particular Key Stage explore – through discussion with teachers of different age groups; the Curriculum Co-ordinator; reading curriculum guides etc. – the range of uses and applications of the chosen resource ;

- implement and evaluate a suggested activity;
- share the findings with other students or possibly with teachers in the appropriate Key Stage.

Relevance of activity for pupils/student teacher

- Learners of mathematics require a wide range of experiences that may incorporate the use of different resources. Seldom does a single introduction to a mathematical idea result in understanding for all!

Useful References

Curriculum Council for Wales (1993) *Using Computers in Primary Mathematics*, Cardiff: CCW.

Activity 8.7: Exploring patterns

PURPOSE OF ACTIVITY:

To develop the student's awareness of the significance of pattern in mathematics.

Task guidelines

INITIAL INPUT:

The mentor should:

- arrange for the student to work with a group of pupils;
- identify and discuss possible patterns that could be explored and described by pupils, i.e. which are appropriate and relevant to a particular aspect of mathematics being studied;
- support the student in planning an appropriate activity.

TASK:

The student should:

- Devise an activity in which pupils are asked to explore and/or describe patterns relating to a particular aspect of mathematical work. Pupils could be asked to describe verbally (and, if appropriate, in writing) a pattern provided by the student, or to create patterns and describe them to each other.

FEEDBACK:

The mentor should discuss:

- the appropriateness of the student's activity;
- the use of resources;
- pupils' difficulties in exploring and articulating visual and numerical patterns.

Patterns could be visual or numerical. Patterns could focus on repetition, relationships, similarities and differences etc. The student might use the environment to discover patterns – see Activity 2. This task could also be linked to identifying, representing and describing patterns in other curriculum areas – for example – in music: exploring, representing and describing patterns in sound.

146

Relevance of activity for pupils/student teacher

- Transposition of visual and numerical patterns into words is a pre-algebra stage and can be used to introduce and establish mathematical language associated with algebra;
- Focusing on patterns demonstrates the creative aspects of mathematics appropriate to primary age pupils.

Useful References:

Bramald, R. (1993) 'A Pattern for Algebra', *Child Education*, Vol 70 (9), pp 14–16.

Brissenden, T. (1988) *Talking about Mathematics: Mathematical Discussion in Primary Classrooms*, Oxford: Basil Blackwell.

Weller, B. (1994) 'Taking the Lid of Algebra', *Junior Education*, Vol 18(4), pp 26–27.

Activity 8.8: Assessing investigative work

PURPOSE OF ACTIVITY:

To enable the student to assess pupils' ability to use and apply mathematics in a relevant area of mathematical study.

Task guidelines

INITIAL INPUT:

The mentor should:

- select or negotiate with the student a mathematical investigation that is relevant to pupils' current area of mathematical study;
- identify a group of pupils with whom the student should work. (The group should provide optimum opportunities for the student to assess pupils' mathematical understanding and skills rather than to manage pupils' behaviour);
- discuss with the student which pupils should be assessed, how the assessment is to be carried out (e.g. the nature of the student's intervention) and what evidence should be collected (i.e. what counts as evidence).

TASK:

The student should:

- discuss the purpose and content of the investigation proposed by – or negotiated with – the mentor;
- revisit the NC programme of study *Using and Applying Mathematics* for the appropriate Key Stage;
- implement the investigation whilst also, for nominated pupils, assessing and recording significant interactions, responses, difficulties and attainment;
- ensure all pupils are enabled to make progress with the investigation.

FEEDBACK:

The mentor should discuss:

- the student's expectations – were they high enough?
- the student's interactions with pupils. Did they enhance/mask/ reveal pupils' ability to use and apply mathematics?

- how the student interpreted, monitored and recorded pupils' interactions, responses and attainment and the appropriateness and relevance of evidence collected;
- the diagnoses made of pupils' difficulties in using and applying mathematics and how the assessment might inform future planning;
- the fundamental importance of assessment as an integral aspect of teaching.

Relevance of activity for pupils/student teacher

- Using and applying mathematics should always be set in the context of other areas of mathematics.

NB Assessment of pupils' ability to use and apply mathematics, while of fundamental importance, can be challenging even for experienced teachers.

Useful References

Burton, L. (1994) *Children Learning Mathematics: Patterns and Relationships*, Hemel Hempsted: Simon and Schuster.

Sanders, S.E. (1994) 'Don't give up on AT1', *Strategies*, Vol 4 (6) pp 26-27.

General Reading:

Atkinson, S. (1992) *Mathematics with Reason*, London: Hodder and Stoughton.

Ball, G. (1990) *Talking and Learning: Primary Mathematics for the National Curriculum,* Hemel Hempsted: Simon and Schuster.

Brissenden, T. (1988) *Talking about Mathematics: Mathematical Discussion in Primary Classrooms*, Oxford: Basil Blackwell.

Curriculum Council for Wales (1991) *Thematic Mathematics in Key Stage 1*, Cardiff: CCW.

Green, D. and Graham,. A. (Eds) (1994) *Data Handling: Teaching with the National Curriculum*, Leamington Spa: Scholastic.

Sawyer, A. (1993) *Developments in Primary Mathematics Teaching*, London: David Fulton.

Shuard, H., Walsh, A., Goodwin, J. and Worcester, V. (1991) *Prime: Calculators, Children and Mathematics*, Hemel Hempsted: Simon and Schuster.

Straker, A. (1993) *Talking Points in Mathematics*, Cambridge: Cambridge University Press.

The Mathematical Association (1992) *Mental Methods in Mathematics: A First Resort,* Leicester: The Mathematical Association

In addition, student teachers might find the following publications useful:

- *Child Education (Scholastic);*
- *Junior Education (Scholastic); and*
- *Mathematics in Schools (The Journal of the Mathematical Association).*

The Mathematical Association and the Association of Teachers of Mathematics also produce materials to support the teaching of mathematics in primary schools.

Section 9

Activities for subject mentoring: science

Activity 9.1: Investigating children's ideas about scientific concepts

PURPOSE OF ACTIVITY:

To develop the student's understanding that children are likely to have formed their own ideas and explanations about everyday *phenomena* which may not always be accurate or helpful to the development of *accepted* scientific understandings.

Task Guidelines

INITIAL INPUT

The mentor should:

- help the student to identify an aspect of science that the pupils will be studying in the near future;
- identify a group of pupils with whom the student can work.

TASK:

The student should:

- devise a simple task (i.e. an interview, a concept map, a drawing, a game etc.) to assess pupils' present understanding of a key concept associated with this aspect of science;
- analyze the pupils' responses.

FEEDBACK:

The mentor should discuss:
- the appropriateness and effectiveness of the task the student devised for eliciting pupils' understandings;
- the discoveries the student made about pupils' ideas and understanding of the concept;
- the implications pupils' understandings would have for teaching this topic;
- the importance of challenging pupils' present understandings and possible ways of going about this.

The aim of this task is not to find out how much information pupils can recall: e.g. how many different animals/insects/birds pupils can name! Rather, the student should try to discover pupils' ideas about, for example, what makes a rolling ball eventually stop, what is inside their bodies etc.

Relevance of activity for pupils/student teacher

- Children will have formed many ideas about the world around them from their own observations, explorations and experiences. These ideas may influence the way in which they interpret their scientific investigations: e.g.:

    blood moves around your body when you wiggle;
    an animal is living because it's got a face;
    forces are big and strong;
    a force is when you're made to do something.

- Simply giving pupils the *correct* explanation is unlikely to change their ideas. Students need to be aware of pupils' likely and actual preconceptions about key concepts and challenge and work from their ideas.

Useful References

Carré, C. and Ovens, C. (1994) *Science 7–11 Developing Primary Teaching Skills*, London: Routledge (See Chapter 3 Restructuring Children's Understandings).

Curriculum Council for Wales (1992) *Starting from Children's Ideas*, Cardiff: CCW.

Comber, M. and Johnson, P. (1995) 'Pushes and Pulls: the potential of concept mapping for assessment', *Primary Science Review*, No 36, pp 10–12.

Sorsby, B. (1991) 'What are things made of? . . . or is this question too hard?', *Primary Science Review*, No 18, pp 22–24.

Watts, M. (1985) 'A study of children's alternative frameworks of the concept of force' in B Hodgson and E Scanlon, (Eds) *Approaching Primary Science*, London: Harper and Row.

Willson, S. and Willson, M. (1994) 'Concept mapping as an assessment tool', *Primary Science Review*, No 34, pp 14–16.

Primary SPACE (Science Processes and Concept Exploration) Project, Research Reports (1990 onwards) Liverpool: Liverpool University Press.

Figure 9.1: Discussing a science project

Activity 9.2: Developing pupils' observation skills

PURPOSE OF ACTIVITY:

To develop the student's understanding of the purpose and significance of observation in science.

Task Guidelines

INITIAL INPUT :

The mentor should:

- help the student to identify an aspect of work currently being undertaken in science and ask the student to collect a set of related *objects*. (Depending on the aspect of science being studied, *objects* could be materials, plants, toys etc. or possibly secondary source material – e.g. photographs.);
- identify a group of pupils with whom the student can work;
- remind the student of any safety issues (e.g. if the student suggests including plants, seeds, food, glass etc. in the collection);
- check whether the student has considered the use of any equipment to enhance observation – e.g. a range of magnifiers such as hand lenses, *midispectors*, simple microscopes (see Science Activity 8).

TASK:

The student should:

- work with a group of pupils helping them to become more focused in their observations: making comparisons, identifying common features, noticing detail etc.

EXTENSION:

Depending on what is being observed and pupils' understanding and previous experiences, the student could help pupils to seek and identify patterns through:

- sorting and setting objects according to observable features, e.g. toys which move by pulling;
- classifying objects (e.g. living/never been alive); or

- ordering objects – focusing on the way the objects change in the sequence, (e.g. increasing size of snail shells, differences in pitch of note as amount of air in bottle is changed.)

FEEDBACK:

The mentor should discuss:

- the appropriateness of the collection of objects in terms of the task – was there sufficient variety? Were the differences in objects evident? Did the objects enable pupils to observe what was expected/required?
- the role the student took when observations were being made;
- the nature of the student's comments and questions and responses to pupils' questions;
- the difficulties pupils had in making comparisons, in sorting, ordering and classifying (e.g.- did pupils have more difficulty finding similarities than finding differences? Could pupils give reasons for particular groupings?).

The student should consider questions that help pupils think about the observations they make. For example, instead of *Which side of the leaf is shiny?* ask *Why do you think the top side of the leaf is shiny?* Instead of *What colour is the shell?* ask *Why do you think the shell is that colour?*

The student could also be asked to think of other ways in which pupils could be encouraged to make more detailed and effective observations (e.g. observing for the purpose of modelling or drawing; identifying objects while blindfolded; limiting the number of objects being observed; describing something to the rest of the class; playing 20 questions; keeping a diary of observations over time etc.).

Relevance of activity for pupils/student teacher

- Observation is the starting point for most scientific investigations;
- Sorting and classifying objects not only encourages pupils to observe more carefully but also to look for patterns. Understanding patterns can help pupils to predict, hypothesize and to explain;
- Student teachers should encourage pupils to focus on *detail* and that which is *relevant*.

155

Useful References

Association for Science Education (1991) (2nd Edn) *Be Safe!* Hatfield: ASE. Chamberlain, V. (1990) 'Developing observation and drawing skills in the infant classroom', *Primary Science Review*, No 12, p18–20.

Harlen, W. and Symington, D. (1985) 'Helping children to observe' in W Harlen (Ed.) *Primary Science: Taking the Plunge*, London: Heinemann.

Activity 9.3: Planning an investigation – is it a fair test?

PURPOSE OF ACTIVITY:

To develop the student's understanding of the concept of a *fair test* and how best s/he can support pupils in planning an investigation.

Task Guidelines

INITIAL INPUT:

The mentor should:

- provide information on pupils' previous work on *fair testing*;
- identify an aspect of pupils' current work in science;
- identify a group of pupils with whom the student can work.

TASK:

The student should:

- devise an activity that will enable her/him to ascertain pupils' present understanding of a *fair test*.

For example, the children could be asked how they could find out who is the best athlete in the school. Pupils could be helped to consider how they would go about this and whether the number of pupils involved, the length of the track/field, the age of the pupils, the number of competitions etc. is important. This should lead to a discussion of what is *fair* and how they could devise a fair test for the above example.

- taking account of pupils' current understanding of the requirements of a fair test, the student should support pupils in planning an investigation in their current topic.

FEEDBACK:

The mentor should discuss:

- the effectiveness of the initial activity devised by the student to ascertain pupils' understanding of a fair test;

- the student's findings (for example, pupils' understanding of which variables are constant, and which particular variable has to be changed or measured);
- pupils' difficulties with fair testing;
- how effectively the student used this information to support pupils in planning an investigation in their current topic.

KS1 pupils should be able to recognize when a test is fair, KS2 pupils should know how to plan and carry out a fair test. Older and more able pupils should be able to discuss *variables* – i.e. the variable that is changed – *independent variable*, those that are observed or measured – *dependent variables* and those that are kept the same – *control variables*.

Pupils should be encouraged to recognize and understand the link between the original purpose of their investigation, the variables that have been changed/measured and the outcome of their investigation. For example:

> I tried to find a way of making sugar dissolve faster. When I changed the temperature (the variable that changes) of the water, the sugar dissolved faster (the variable that is measured: time). I can draw a graph which shows the relationship between time and temperature of water.

Relevance of activity for pupils/ student teacher

- The concept of a fair test forms a central part of pupils' ability to devise investigations. Through investigations pupils can be helped to develop their scientific knowledge and understanding;
- Children may need help in deciding what variables to change, measure and keep the same when devising their investigation. They will also need to carry out investigations in a range of different contexts in order to help them fully understand the concept of a fair test.

Useful References

Goldsworthy, A. and Feasey, R. (1994) *Making Sense of Primary Science Investigations*, Hatfield: ASE. (This book is strongly recommended to support investigatory work.)

Harlen, W. (1993) (2nd. Edition) *Teaching and Learning Primary Science*, London: Paul Chapman. (Pp 63–66, Investigating)

Twiss, S. (1995) 'Using cards to help children order their thoughts', *Primary Science Review*, No 36, pp 12–13.

Activities 9.4 & 9.5: Taking and recording measurements (9.4); and Interpreting data (9.5)

PURPOSE OF ACTIVITIES:

To develop the student's understanding of how to support pupils in taking and recording measurements and in interpreting the data collected.

Task guidelines

INITIAL INPUT:

The mentor should:

- identify an aspect of science work currently being undertaken and guide the student's planning of a simple exploration/investigation/ survey that requires measurements to be taken;
- discuss possible methods of keeping ongoing records that are appropriate to the task.

TASK:

The student should:

- devise and implement an activity that requires measurements to be taken over a limited period of time. (Where appropriate the student should be encouraged to make use of IT, e.g. data handling programmes);
- help pupils to make sense of and interpret the data they have collected.

FEEDBACK:

After completing tasks 4 and 5, the mentor should discuss:

- the relevance and appropriateness of the task;
- how far the method of recording adopted was appropriate to the task and pupils' understanding;
- the accuracy of pupils' readings and recordings (and reasons for their difficulties);
- what support pupils needed and to what extent this was given;
- why it is important for pupils to record results systematically;

- whether the student helped pupils to organize or classify the information gathered in order that pupils could most easily identify patterns or sequences;
- how easily the pupils were able to identify patterns, and make hypotheses and predictions based on the evidence collected. (Were the pupils willing to change their ideas in the face of the evidence provided?)

Relevance of activity for pupils/student teacher

- Taking and recording measurements are important aspects of undertaking scientific investigations;
- Through interpreting data – seeking and identifying patterns – children come to understand important scientific relationships;
- Making use of IT allows pupils to manipulate findings in ways that make it easier for them to identify patterns.

IN RECORDING MEASUREMENTS PUPILS WILL MOVE FROM:

- completing ready prepared tables; to
- drawing up their own tables suggested by the teacher; to
- considering and drawing up the most appropriate means of collecting data.

SUGGESTIONS OF FORMS OF ONGOING RECORDS:

- *tally charts* – of numbers of flowers of a particular kind in a habitat; how often particular sounds are heard on a walk;
- *tables* – of weather records or temperature readings;
- *diaries* – of changes in a horse chestnut tree during the course if a year;
- *informal notes for later reference* – on observations of the way woodlice and snails move;
- *drawings* – of metal objects found in the classroom.

STUDENTS COULD HELP PUPILS TO CONSIDER THE FOLLOWING IN TAKING AND RECORDING MEASUREMENTS:

- How will measurements be taken?
- What equipment is needed/most appropriate?
- How often will measurements need to be taken?
- How many times do measurements need to be repeated?
- How will ongoing measurements be recorded? (e.g. diagrams, tables, database, sequence of pictures, personal notes.)
- What form of recording is most appropriate ?

IN INTERPRETING THE DATA, STUDENTS MAY NEED TO HELP PUPILS TO CONSIDER:

- Does the data need to be classified or organized in any way in order that patterns and relationships can easily be identified?
- Are there any patterns visible? (Patterns could be relationships between, for example, length of shadows and time of day, pitch and length of vibrating material, distance travelled and type of surface etc. or characteristics common to all animals, insects, metals etc.)
- Can pupils use the data to give explanations (hypotheses), make predictions and draw conclusions?

N.B. – On occasions it is useful for pupils to attempt to interpret and make sense of data from secondary sources. Students could therefore also devise an activity that makes use of secondary data e.g. newspaper reports of world-wide weather conditions, findings from other pupils' investigations etc. This will encourage pupils to consider the actual findings and help them to rely on data from a range of contexts.

Useful References

Elliott, P. and Pratt, D. (1993) 'Investigating skin temperature – a novel use of the spreadsheet', *Primary Science Review*, No 28, pp 19–21.

Frost, R. (1993) *IT in Primary Science*, Hatfield: ASE.

Goldsworthy, A. and Feasey, R. (1994) *Making Sense of Primary Science Investigations*, Hatfield: ASE.

Green, D. and Graham, A. (Eds.) (1994) *Data Handling: Teaching with the National Curriculum*, Leamington Spa: Scholastic.

In addition:

Primary Science Review (1995), No 40, is dedicated to IT and science.

Figure 9.2: Interpreting scientific data

Activity 9.6: Encouraging and responding to pupils' questions

PURPOSE OF ACTIVITY:

To develop the student's understanding of the importance and nature of pupil questioning in science and of appropriate ways of responding to pupils' questions.

Task Guidelines

INITIAL INPUT:

The mentor should:

- discuss the importance of encouraging pupils to ask questions and in particular questions that are supportive of their scientific understanding;
- discuss strategies and appropriate stimuli for encouraging pupils' questions: e.g. question board, 20 questions, *What am I?* game, question box;
- model for the student the process of implementing a practical investigation.

TASK:

The student should:

- focus on the kinds of questions pupils raise and how the teacher responds to these;
- make note of pupils' questions (particularly of questions which s/he would find challenging) and consider how s/he might have responded to these;
- work with a further group of pupils, focusing her/his attention on pupils' questions and their responses.

FEEDBACK:

The mentor should discuss:

- how far the student felt s/he managed to support pupils' questioning in relation to developing scientific understanding;
- strategies for encouraging and responding to pupils' questions.

Students need to learn how to deal with pupils' questions that they are unable to answer or where the scientific explanation may be beyond pupils' present level of understanding. Where this is the case students may find it beneficial to draw pupils' attention to:

- significant features – What can you see . . . ?
- comparisons – Is that the same as . . . ?
- relationships – Is there any connection between . . . and . . . ?
- the influence of variables – Would it make a difference if you changed . . . ? and
- possible investigations – What do you think would happen if you. . . . ?

Relevance of activity for pupils/student teacher

Questions form the link between previous and new understandings.

Students need to understand the importance of the following in relation to questioning in science:

- encouraging reasoning based on evidence rather than guessing;
- of moving pupils' questions towards a form that can lead to investigations;
- of keeping the discussion/questions tied to the action;
- of helping pupils to break down their questions into more manageable parts;
- of encouraging pupils to think further for themselves, e.g. why do you think . . . ?
- of encouraging pupils' questions even if these questions cannot be answered.

Useful References

Harlen, W. (1993) (2nd Edition) *Teaching and Learning Primary Science*, (pp 83–91 Questioning), London: Paul Chapman.

Jarman, R. (1991) *Questioning: An Important Science Skill*, Queens University, Belfast, ASE/ICI/NIESU.

Jelly, S. (1985) 'Helping children raise questions – and answering them' in W Harlen (Ed.) *Primary Science: Taking the Plunge*, London: Heinemann.

Woodward, C. (1993) 'Pupils' Questions – the whys and hows', *Questions*, Vol 5, No 7, pp 23–24.

Activity 9.7: Communicating findings

PURPOSE OF ACTIVITY:

To encourage the student to consider the variety of ways in which pupils can communicate the findings of their investigations.

Task Guidelines

INITIAL INPUT:

This activity could lead on from activities 4 and 5. Alternatively the student could make use of findings gathered in a recent investigation or from a secondary source.

The mentor should:

- help the student to identify an appropriate set of findings;
- help the student to recognize the range of possible audiences: e.g. teacher, pupils in another class, whole school, parents, local newspaper, industrial company etc.;
- identify a group of pupils with whom the student can work.

TASK:

The student should:

- support pupils in devising appropriate ways of communicating their findings;
- help pupils to clarify their understanding through their chosen means of communication and to evaluate the appropriateness and effectiveness of their work.

FEEDBACK:

The mentor should discuss:

- how far the chosen method supported pupils' understanding in science (or was it simply an exercise in descriptive writing?).

Findings could be communicated through discussion, talk, tape/audio recording, letters to other people advising on findings, pictures, class assembly, newspaper report, poster, PE/drama, model making, lists of instructions etc. The student should consider whether there is an opportunity to make use of it.

Relevance of activity for pupils /student teacher

- In order to communicate their findings pupils need to summarize and reflect on their experiences;
- Communicating the results of their investigations to a known audience also makes their work more meaningful to pupils.

Useful References

de Boo, M. (1988) Recording work in science: using words', *Primary Science Review*, No 7, pp 12–14.

Howard, S. (1992) Using the performing arts as a medium for scientific concept development in primary school children', *Primary Science Review*, No 25, pp 28–29.

Keogh, B. and Naylor, S. (1993) 'Learning in science: another way in', *Primary Science Review*, No 26, pp 22–23.

Malcolm, R. (1990) 'Let's make a record', *Primary Science Review*, No 15, pp 14–16.

Newton, L. (1988) 'Children recording in primary science', *Primary Science Review*, No 6, pp 8–9.

Paterson, V. (1987) 'What might be learnt from children's writing in primary science? *Primary Science Review*, No 4, pp 17–20.

Activity 9.8: Using scientific equipment

PURPOSE OF ACTIVITY:

To raise the student's awareness of the importance of safety issues in science teaching.

Task Guidelines

INITIAL INPUT:

The mentor should:

- help the student to select a piece of equipment that may be significant to pupils' future investigations. This could be for example, a hand lens, a metre rule, weighing scales, a Newton meter, magnets, a measuring jug/cylinder, a thermometer, a stop watch, a tocker timer, droppers etc.;
- identify a group of pupils with whom the student can work.

TASK:

The student should:

- devise an activity in order to teach pupils how to use this equipment correctly and safely.

FEEDBACK:

The mentor should discuss:

- the relevance of the activity the student devised;
- how the activity was structured, managed and organized;
- whether the student appropriately emphasized safety issues;
- how the pupils' skills and understandings could be incorporated into an investigation.

Relevance of activity for pupils/student teacher

- Pupils need to learn how to use equipment accurately and safely if they are to be effective in carrying out investigations;
- There is a need to teach some specific skills in isolation before incorporating these skills into a whole investigation.

Useful References

Association for Science Education, (1991) (2nd Edition) *Be Safe!*, Hatfield: ASE.

General Reading

Carlton, K. and Parkinson, E. (1994) *Physical Sciences: A Primary Teacher's Guide*, London: Cassell.

Carré, C. and Ovens, C. (1994) Science 7-11, *Developing Primary Teaching Skills*, London: Routledge.

Curriculum Council for Wales (1991) *Aspects of Science for Primary Teachers: Earth in Space*, Cardiff: CCW.

Curriculum Council For Wales (1992) *Aspects of Science for Primary Teachers: Light and Sound*, Cardiff: CCW.

Curriculum Council for Wales (1992) *Aspects of Science for Primary Teachers: Energy*, Cardiff: CCW.

Farrow, S. (1996) *The Really Useful Science Book: A Framework of Knowledge for Primary Teachers*, London: Falmer Press.

Peacock, G. and Smith, R. (1994) (2nd Edition) *Teaching and Understanding Science*, London: Hodder and Stoughton.

Wenham, M. (1995) *Understanding Primary Science: Ideas, Concepts and Explanations*, London: Paul Chapman Publishing.

Section 10

Materials for Professional Development

10.1: Introduction

The materials in this section derive from the piloting of six of the activities outlined in Sections 7, 8 and 9 – two for each of the core subjects of English, Mathematics and Science. Many of the mentors were observed as they worked with their student teachers and at a later stage both mentors and student teachers were interviewed. In these interviews we wished to ascertain opinions about the value and effectiveness of the activities. In addition, subject mentors involved in this project kept a journal of their work in schools – noting down their own, their student teachers' and their colleagues' responses.

But the comments recorded in this section are not simply reports of how activities were implemented within different schools. Rather, they aim to highlight key themes or issues that are likely to be of significance to the success of subject mentoring. Some accounts give examples of how activities were used effectively by mentors. Others point to some of the challenges faced by student teachers in implementing their tasks, or to students' lack of understanding of good practice within particular subject areas. Yet other accounts highlight the challenges of managing and organizing subject mentoring within schools, and to the significance of dialogue between schools and HEIs.

Each account is followed by a number of related questions. It is intended that these questions are used to initiate reflection and discussion on the possibilities and challenges of mentoring subject knowledge in the primary school. This process is seen as of fundamental importance if schools are to be effective in developing student teachers' knowledge, understanding and skills in the teaching of the core curriculum. Materials in this section could, therefore, be used for personal reflection and consideration by individual teachers or for promoting discussion amongst groups of teachers, amongst the whole staff or between schools and their partner HEIs.

It should be noted that many of the issues highlighted here are addressed earlier in *The Principles and Processes of Mentoring*. In reading Section 10, therefore, you might like to refer back to the relevant sections in Part A of this handbook.

You should also read the corresponding activities in sections 7–9. These are:

ENGLISH:

- Activity 7.5 – Spelling;
- Activity 7.8 – Story Writing (narrative).

MATHEMATICS:

- Activity 8.1 – Using a mathematical game;
- Activity 8.4 – Check the Rumour.

SCIENCE:

- Activity 9.1 – Investigating children's ideas about scientific concepts;
- Activity 9.2 – Developing pupils' observation skills.

10.2: Activity 7.5: Spelling

The following comments were made by the class mentor and her student teacher after piloting this activity.
The class mentor:

> The purpose of this activity, I think, is to draw the student's attention to the kind of spelling mistakes children commonly make. We need to remember that spelling has got to be taught. In the debriefing session I wanted to help the student realize that there are families of words and that children tend to make common spelling errors.
>
> It would help to know what work the student has done in college on this. If we're teaching them one theory and the college is teaching them another. . . ! Actually, we'd like some direction here. In our school we haven't got a spelling policy yet.

The student teacher:

> The purpose of this activity is to help me focus on the strategies pupils might resort to when they come across words they can't spell and the strategies I can use to help them with their spelling. To be honest, my priority at the moment is on the strategies I can use – with experience I can look at the wide varieties of strategies the children use. Also, it is difficult to focus on what the pupils are doing when you are meant to be teaching as well. One child in particular required a lot of my time. I think I would have got more from this activity if I had been given time to observe the children – because I'm there they tend to use me as a tool too.
>
> I was given this activity near the end of my teaching practice and it's made me realize that I've been far too focused on making sure the children's spelling is perfect for the final draft of their work. Really, I should have been looking much more closely at families of words and devising strategies and games to improve the pupils' ability with spelling.

These accounts highlight several important issues: that of *partnership* between schools and HEIs; the management of subject mentoring; and also student teachers' common difficulties:

- In relation to subject mentoring, what are the respective roles and responsibilities of schools and HEIs? What other issues need to be discussed or negotiated? What contribution could HEIs make to the professional development of teachers?
- If subject mentoring is to be effective then it appears that students may need to be given the time and space to *observe* (pupils and teachers), to work with small groups of pupils and to reflect on their experiences. What implications does this have for how students' school-based work is managed and organized?
- Why do student teachers commonly seem concerned with their own teaching – that is, with *useful* teaching strategies and with being seen as a *good* teacher? How can students be helped to focus on the process of pupil learning?

10.3: Activity 7.8: Story writing (narrative)

The following extracts are taken from a journal kept by one subject mentor who was working with a PGCE student on placement in her school. The student was at the beginning of his second and final block teaching experience. These extracts show how the subject mentor used this activity as the basis of her work with the student over a period of several weeks and how links were made between ITT and the further professional development of teachers.

May 8th

The student teacher was invited to attend an INSET session I was running for colleagues, in which I emphasized the importance of providing pupils with a range of writing opportunities. In particular I discussed ways of introducing one form of narrative writing – stylistic modelling. This strategy was demonstrated using several texts appropriate for pupils at Key Stages 1 and 2.

May 19th

I suggested that the student, who was working in a Y5 class, might use stylistic modelling to produce picture books for the Reception class. I recommended that the student use the text *Where Does the Brown Bear Go?* by Nicky Weiss. I discussed this task with the student and suggested that initially he should read the story to the class, talking about the author's use of rhythm, rhyme and patterns of language. This should be followed by a brainstorming session in which the pupils are asked to think about possible settings and related language. I explained to the student that only then are the pupils ready to attempt to write and illustrate their own texts.

May 26th

The student carried out the task – helping the children to sort out their ideas and shape them into an appropriate form. There was an excellent response from the children once they had produced an initial successful verse. The student was helped to understand that redrafting should involve the pupils in consideration of issues such as tense, appropriate adjectives, number of syllables, the use of language and context.

HALF-TERM

June 4th – 16th

The student has received a lot of support during this period. He was shown how to make the books and how to organize, assist and stimulate the children. He needed to be shown how to intervene to keep the children on task. The children were very interested in this activity and they took great pride in their work. Some lovely books were produced.

- What different aspects of teachers' knowledge did the mentor focus on?
- What were the student's apparent difficulties with this task? How did the mentor appear to support the student?

Figure 10.1: Story writing with young pupils

10.4: Activity 8.1: Using a mathematical game

Two mentors chose to use the mathematical game *Show Me* which was included in a pack produced by West Glamorgan LEA (CSMIS) for a *number and algebra* course they were running.

In this game each child is given the digit cards 0–9. The children arrange the digit cards on the table in front of them and are then asked (by the teacher or another pupil) to *show me* the appropriate card or cards in response to a question. For example, they may be asked to:

- Show me a number more than 5 but less than 10; or
- Show me 36 divided by 6.

In one school, while the class mentor observed the student teacher, it was the subject mentor who carried out the feedback session. The class mentor made the following comments after observing the student teacher carrying out the task:

> The student should have concentrated on consolidating pupils' understanding of number bonds to ten, rather than moving on to use higher numbers.
>
> The game lasted for 40 minutes and was too *drawn out*.
>
> The student's questions needed to focus more closely on helping the pupils to talk about the strategies they were using – although I found it difficult to monitor all the student's questions while also teaching the rest of the class.

In the feedback session the subject mentor aimed to help the student to evaluate his own teaching and also discussed the comments that had been made by the class mentor. She states:

> The student maintained that he enjoyed the activity and found the resources very easy to make and organize. He felt that the children were highly stimulated by the activity and the fact that they did not need to record anything was a motivating factor.
>
> The student commented that he was aware of his class mentor's views with respect to consolidating the pupil's understanding of number bonds to ten but felt that the more able children were eager to play with higher numbers. He therefore decided to capitalize on their enthusiasm. The student did not agree with the

class mentor's view that the activity was too *drawn out* as the children did not appear at all restless or bored and were still eager to carry on playing the game at the end of the session. He feels that decisions about the duration of this activity should be judged according to the pupils' enthusiasm.

The student maintained that this activity allowed him to pose more open questions to the children and that he did question them about their methods. This gave him an insight into their thinking and allowed him to diagnose individual strengths and weaknesses. Being asked to make the highest/lowest numbers using two digit cards also helped to reinforce the concept of place value with the most able children.

The subject mentor then made the following suggestions (to the class mentor and student teacher):

The student should consider the use of mathematical language carefully and plan to develop this in context.

The *Show Me* game could be extended in a variety of ways. For example by using a limited number of digit cards. The student could ask pupils:

- How many different numbers can you make using the digits . . .?
- What are the smallest/largest numbers you can make using the digits . . .?
- Using only the digits . . . and the symbols + − and = make the following numbers . . .;
- What is the largest number you can make using the digits . . . and -, +, x and ÷ Use your calculator to help you.

In this school, both the subject mentor and class mentor were directly involved in working with the student teacher:

- What role does the subject mentor adopt?
- What aspects of the student's knowledge and understanding are they each trying to develop?
- What are the benefits of organizing subject mentoring in this way?
- Can you foresee any possible difficulties − e.g. in terms of relationships with colleagues? If so, how might these be overcome?

Figure 10.2: Using a mathematical game

10.5: Activity 8.4: Check the rumour

Most mentors who piloted this activity were very enthusiastic about the learning opportunities it provided – both for their student teachers and their pupils! However, whilst initially this seemed a fairly straightforward and simple task, several students did find it quite challenging.

One student working with a Y6 class suggested that the pupils investigate the rumour *all shapes that have the same area also have the same perimeter*. The senior mentor writes:

> Initially I encouraged the student to give his ideas on what an investigation involves. He seemed quite clear on the nature of an open-ended investigation. However, he appeared reluctant to attempt one with the class. He seemed to want to guide the children more than I felt was necessary. He agreed to allow the children the freedom to decide how they would tackle the investigation. Ultimately he acknowledged that this had been the right decision but admitted that at times he had felt rather intimidated because the activity appeared to be led by the pupils rather than him . . .

Another student, told his Y5 pupils *there is a rumour that most of the cars in the car-park are red*. This student's class mentor writes:

> I discussed the idea of an investigation with the student – he was unsure about what this involved but was very keen to try out any ideas. I told him to have a variety of resources available for the children to record their findings and allow them to decide which of the resources it is most appropriate to use. He wanted to give the pupils graph paper and I said the graph paper should be available but he should allow the pupils the opportunity to make the decision . . .

- What did these student teachers find challenging about implementing this activity?
- What did they need to understand?
- How would you support them in developing this understanding?

One student, who was aiming to develop pupils' understanding of measures, told her Y1 class that she had heard the rumour *three times round your head is the same as your height.* In her evaluation this student was openly critical of this activity. She wrote:

> This activity took up about half an hour of my time in which I had to devote myself exclusively to just two children. It was difficult to persuade the other Y1 children to try to continue their set work (another investigation) without disturbing my activity. However, we all achieved what we set out to do and it proved a very enjoyable exercise for myself and the two pupils involved.
>
> The children worked methodically and logically, they knew that it would be easier to wrap one short piece of paper around their heads and then make two more pieces the same length, rather than trying to use one very long piece of paper. I vaguely hinted at the use of string without actually mentioning the word, but this was not picked up on.
>
> These sorts of investigations seem to be very useful in allowing teachers to assess the capabilities of individual children and to look at their ways of thinking. Provided that other children in the class are capable of working alone and unwatched, those participating in the activity can be exposed to meaningful and investigative mathematics.

- Are her criticisms valid?
- What should this student be helped to consider?

10.6: Activity 9.1: Investigating children's ideas about scientific concepts

This activity was piloted with several students at different stages of their professional preparation and who were following both PGCE and BA(Ed) courses.

One student in her third year of a BA(Ed) was beginning her block teaching experience in a mixed aged class (Years 4, 5 and 6) of 26 children. As the cross-curricular topic for the half-term was *space*, the student decided to explore pupils' understanding of two ideas: *What is the Sun?* and *How does the Sun behave in relation to the Earth?*

The student chose to initiate a discussion with the pupils, initially asking them, *What can you tell me about the sun?* In the feedback discussion the student was helped to consider the significance of the pupils' comments and eventually came to the following conclusions:

- Children will have developed their own ideas in an attempt to make sense of the world around them;
- Some of children's ideas are totally understandable in that they are based on first hand observations – e.g. the sun goes round the earth;
- Being aware of children's preconceptions is important if teachers are to help pupils to *move forward* in their understanding;
- A class of 26 children do not have 26 different ideas;
- Being aware of children's preconceptions will affect the way activities are structured and the nature of the teacher's interaction with pupils. It does not mean that the teacher needs to plan individual science activities for every pupil.
- Do you agree with these statements?
- What implications do they have for subject mentoring?

Another student teacher on her final block teaching experience was working with a class of Y2 pupils. In preparation for future work on the topic *the sea-shore* she asked the children, *How does the sand get on to beaches?* This is a transcript of the pupils' responses. This student maintained that she didn't really learn anything from this discussion:

Student: 'How does the sand get on to beaches?'

Pupil 1: 'From a factory. Men bring it in plastic bags and dump it on the beach.'

Pupil 2: 'No that's not right. It was there before we were born and there was no electricity in that time.'

Pupil 3: 'Sand is just natural. It's been there all the time and has never moved.'

Pupil 4: 'But if God made the sand then why are there shells and pebbles? That's what makes the sand . . .'

Pupil 5: 'The sea hit the rocks to turn it into sand . . .'

Pupil 4: 'The sea hits the rocks, the rocks hit the shells and the shells break up into sand . . .'

Pupil 6: '. . . The pebbles and shells hit the rocks and then turn them into tiny pieces.'

Pupil 1: 'But how do the pebbles get to the sea-side?'

Pupil 6: 'Miss, can we throw a rock into the sea and watch if it turns into sand?'

- If you were working with this student, what would you want her to consider and to understand?
- How would you go about this?

Figure 10.3: Investigating children's ideas about a scientific concept

10.7: Activity 9.2: Developing pupils' observation skills

A PGCE student piloted this activity with a Y5 class. It is interesting to compare the nature of the comments made by the class mentor and student teacher and their evaluations of this lesson.

The class mentor writes:

> The purpose of the activity was discussed with the student in advance, and we decided to use mini-beasts as the main focus of the observation. The student was encouraged to research the topic for himself and to carefully consider what resources he would need.
>
> The student was well prepared for the activity. He had considered the use of apparatus carefully, provided science keys and discussed hygiene and the care of insects. The children were given bug-boxes and taken into the nature area to find mini-beasts. I felt the student needed to work more closely with the children instead of searching for his own specimens. I therefore took an active role in the lesson and highlighted places the children would be likely to find insects. I asked the children *prompt* questions in order to encourage the student to participate more. For example, I asked the pupils, *Why do you think insects are likely to be found in damp areas?*
>
> When the children had collected their specimens we returned to the classroom. The student encouraged the children to look closely using hand lenses and to try and identify each insect. I did suggest the children use encyclopaedias to help them identify and find out more about the species – and develop their research skills as well!
>
> The student did spend rather a long time encouraging the children to look closely at the insects and I did feel some of the motivation was lost. I therefore suggested that the children should make some observational drawings of the insects . . .

The student teacher writes:

> For this activity I focused on the importance of observation as

a stimulus for learning and investigation. The activity was completed by a group of five children who used magnifying equipment to observe a collection of mini-beasts from the nature area. They then drew pictures of one or two of the mini-beasts and used a classification key and reference books to identify them.

The activity was a success. I attempted to re-direct children's questions to the mini-beasts' observable features and to possible investigations that could be carried out. I felt I was well prepared to do this effectively.

An activity such as this would need careful planning and preparation concerning the student's own knowledge of the objects/animals being observed. At the same time it is important that the student is able to apply a style of questioning/explanation which would encourage pupils to think 'investigatively' and concentrate on observable features.

It would perhaps be advantageous for a student to observe this type of activity being carried out by a teacher, particularly regarding organization of the remainder of the class who would have to carry out a *non-teacher demanding* activity.

- What role did the class mentor adopt while the student was carrying out this task?
- On the basis of this account, what knowledge/understandings/ skills does the student need to develop?
- How would you go about supporting this student?

Section Reference

Weiss, N. (1990) *Where Does the Brown Bear Go?*, London: Picture Puffins (Penguin Books Ltd).

10.8: Useful References – Mentoring in Initial Teacher Training

Fish, D. (1995) *Quality Mentoring for Student Teachers: A Principled Approach to Practice*, London: David Fulton Press.

Furlong, J. and Maynard, T. (1995) *Mentoring Student Teachers: The Growth of Professional Knowledge*, London: Routledge.

Kerry, T. and Shelton Mayes, A. (1995) *Issues in Mentoring*, London: Routledge.

McIntyre, D. and Hagger, H. (1996) (Eds.) *Mentors in Schools: Developing the Profession of Teaching*, London: David Fulton.

McIntyre, D., Hagger, H. and Wilkin, M. (1993) *Mentoring: Perspectives on School-based Teacher Education*, London: Kogan Page.

Tomlinson. P. (1995) *Understanding Mentoring*, Buckingham: Open University Press.

Wilkin, M. (Ed) (1992) *Mentoring in Schools*, London: Kogan Page.

'Subject-based mentoring in the Primary School' Project

Project Steering Committee

Bob Evans (WO)
John Furlong (UWS)
Trisha Maynard (UWS)
David Robinson (WO)
Sue Sanders (UWS)

(September 1994–June 1995)
Chris Abbott (OHMCI)

(June 1995 – December 1995)
Gareth Wyn Jones (OHMCI)

Subject Groups

ENGLISH
Gill Harper-Jones (UWS)
Gill Lloyd (Tairgwaith Primary School)
Jenny Shanahan (Cilffriw Primary School)

WELSH
Pamela John (Y G Lonlas)
Brin Jones (UWS)
Hefina Morris (Y Login Fach)

MATHEMATICS
Louise James (Pontarddulais Primary School)
Margo Popham (Manselton Primary School)
Sue Sanders (UWS)

SCIENCE
Ian Hill (LEA)
Pat Way (St Joseph's Cathedral Junior School, Swansea)
Catherine Woodward (UWS)

PROJECT DIRECTORS:
John Furlong, Trisha Maynard and Sue Sanders

RESEARCH OFFICER:
Trisha Maynard

Index